For more than a decade, I have seen Dr. Richard Cash's work transform classrooms as I have worked in urban, suburban, and rural settings. What makes his approach so impactful is its practicality—it meets the realities of today's classrooms with strategies that truly work. In this powerful new publication, Dr. Cash places self-regulation at the very heart of student achievement. Grounded in research and built around four essential phases of learning—building confidence, setting goals, monitoring progress, and reflecting on outcomes—this book provides educators with a clear and actionable framework. It empowers teachers to guide students toward becoming focused, resilient, and self-directed learners who not only persist through challenges but take full ownership of their learning journey.

—**Brian Orrenma**, Chief of Academic Affairs, Buckeye Valley Local Schools, Ohio

As a middle school educator who has worked with Dr. Richard Cash since 2014, I've come to trust his work as both practical and inspiring. His strategies have helped me support students in becoming more reflective, independent learners, something every teacher hopes to nurture. Whether you're new to the classroom or have been teaching for years, *Strategies and Tools for Self-Regulation in the Classroom* offers thoughtful and doable ideas that truly make a difference. Tools like reflection prompts, goal-setting exercises, note-taking guides, and strategies for working with peers are easy to weave into the day, and over time, they help students build habits that last well beyond your classroom.

—**Stephanie Vance**, Teacher, North Star Academy, Redwood City School District, California

Strategies and Tools for Self-Regulation in the Classroom brings theory into action by delivering on strategies that impact the four phases of learning. Dr. Cash's simple and practical approach to his strategies and tools will help any teacher, regardless of their experience, feel confident in their ability to positively influence students' skills for self-regulation. This practical guide is needed now more than ever as today's educators navigate the unique learning attitudes, abilities, and needs of every student who enters their classrooms.

—**Josh Lyons, Ed.D.**, Associate Superintendent of Teaching and Learning, Solon Community School District, Iowa

In *Strategies and Tools for Self-Regulation in the Classroom*, Dr. Richard Cash addresses educators' need for practical implementation, offering evidence-based strategies and tools that are both effective and easy to integrate into daily classroom routines. While there is review of theoretical concepts here, the book stands out as a resource for teachers seeking actionable methods to guide students in developing vital self-regulation skills. Its practical structure, organized around four phases of learning, ensures that teachers can readily find and apply techniques, supplemented by ready-to-use activities and reproducible graphic organizers. I look forward to sharing this invaluable resource with our entire faculty and anticipate significant positive shifts in student engagement and ownership over their learning!

—**Amy Schroff, Ed.D.**, Head of Academics, Bishop DuBourg High School, St. Louis, Missouri

Strategies and Tools for Self-Regulation in the Classroom

Boost Student Focus and Meet Learning Goals

RICHARD M. CASH, Ed.D.

Library of Congress Cataloging-in-Publication Data
This book has been filed with the Library of Congress.
LCCN: 2025019477
ISBN: 979-8-88554-984-4

Creative Dramatics activities Space Walk, Space Walk—Give and Take, R.O.L.E., and Dr. Know-It-All on pages 12–15 are adapted from *The Second City Guide to Improv in the Classroom* by Katherine McKnight and Mary Scruggs. San Francisco, CA: Jossey-Bass, 2008. Used with permission. Creative Dramatics activities Ad Game and Think Fast! on pages 13 and 14 are from *Advancing Differentiation: Thinking and Learning for the 21st Century* by Richard M. Cash. Minneapolis, MN: Free Spirit Publishing, 2017. Used with permission. The Gist Method on page 71 is from *Literacy and Learning Centers for the Big Kids, Grades 4–12*, by K.S. McKnight. Engaging Learners, LLC., 2017. Used with permission. The Four Levels of Questions on page 79 are from *Differentiation for Gifted Learners: Going Beyond the Basics* by Diane Heacox and Richard M. Cash, copyright © 2020. Used with permission. The Seven Critical Questioning Strategies on page 80 are adapted from *Advancing Differentiation: Thinking and Learning for the 21st Century* by Richard M. Cash. 2017. Used with permission.

Edited by Cassie Labriola-Sitzman
Cover and interior design by Colleen Pidel

Printed by: 590835
Printed in: China

Free Spirit Publishing
An imprint of Teacher Created Materials
9850 51st Avenue North, Suite 100
Minneapolis, MN 55442
(612) 338-2068
help4kids@freespirit.com
freespirit.com

Dedication

To my husband, Craig Feltmann, thank you for putting up with me during the process of writing this book. Your support and encouragement show in this work.
To my dear sister, Susan Swinick, thank you for your undying love and friendship and for "keeping me in line."

Acknowledgments

Thank you to my colleagues who contributed lesson ideas for this book: Katherine McKnight, Ph.D., Erik Francis, M.Ed., M.S., Dana Schmidt, David Michael Slater, and Katherine McCoy. And to my editor, Cassie Labriola-Sitzman, I truly appreciate you making me look good on paper!

Contents

List of Figures

Introduction

In an ever-evolving world, the ability to learn effectively and independently is indispensable. Our educational systems, while rich in information, often overlook a critical aspect of learning: self-regulation. *Self-regulation* refers to a set of skills that empower students to take charge of their learning, set goals, manage their emotions, and reflect on their progress.

Self-regulation is a cornerstone of effective learning in today's complex educational landscape. As we navigate the post-pandemic era, embrace technological advancements, and address the rising tide of anxiety, stress, and trauma, we can't lose sight of the critical need to foster self-regulation skills. The concerted efforts of educators, institutions, and families to equip students with the ability to manage their feelings, behaviors, and thinking will empower them to overcome challenges, achieve their goals, and thrive.

Self-regulation for learning (SRL) influences various aspects of a learner's life, from academic performance to personal development. Self-regulated learners tend to be more motivated, resilient, and adaptable, making them better equipped to handle challenges as they arise. They also possess the ability to sift through data, prioritize tasks, and stay focused, helping them navigate the information overload of today's connected and fast-paced world while staying on track to achieve their objectives.

Strategies and Tools for Self-Regulation in the Classroom aims to provide you with tools and techniques you can use to enhance learners' capacities to self-regulate, boosting their success in the classroom and beyond.

The ABCs of Self-Regulation

SRL is the process by which learners control their **A**ffect, **B**ehavior, and **C**ognition to achieve learning goals. These are the ABCs of learning, and you'll find them referenced often throughout the strategies in this book.

Affect refers to the emotional aspects of self-regulation, including feelings, moods, and attitudes that influence learning. Positive affect, such as enthusiasm and interest, can enhance motivation and engagement, while negative affect, such as anxiety or frustration, can hinder learning processes.

Behavioral regulation within the classroom involves the actions and habits that learners engage in to achieve the learning objectives. It includes managing time, organizing resources, and maintaining a conducive learning environment.

Cognitive regulation encompasses the mental processes involved in learning, such as attention, memory, and problem-solving. Developing these cognitive skills is essential for effective self-regulation.

These three dimensions of SRL are tightly interwoven and, in self-regulated learners, work in tandem.

The Four Phases of Learning

Learning is a dynamic and multifaceted process that can be broken down into four key phases:

1. Building confidence for learning
2. Setting and managing learning goals
3. Monitoring and adjusting learning techniques
4. Reviewing and reflecting on learning

Understanding and implementing these phases can significantly enhance students' learning experiences and outcomes, which is why the strategies in these pages are structured around these four learning phases.

Students develop greater self-efficacy and positive self-beliefs when they can successfully engage through the learning process. This four-phase cyclical process also enhances students' self-regulation for learning, since each phase requires different skills and techniques.

Why This Book

When I wrote *Self-Regulation in the Classroom: Helping Students Learn How to Learn* in 2016, it was a pioneering book on the theory of SRL. It delves deeply into the theoretical underpinnings and practical applications of SRL, offering educators a comprehensive resource to enhance their teaching strategies. From the feedback I received, it became clear that educators found the theoretical insights valuable, but they sought a more straightforward approach for practical implementation. They wanted clear strategies and tools to help students develop self-regulation skills in the classroom, in real time.

Strategies and Tools for Self-Regulation in the Classroom delivers just that. While the book can be used independently, I advise that you review *Self-Regulation in the Classroom* for a sound understanding of the background and fundamentals of self-regulation for learning. This builds a solid foundation from which you can adapt the strategies in this book to your specific classroom environment and student needs.

This book is designed for educators working in grades 3–12, as well as anyone interested in enhancing students' learning processes. Whether you have a student struggling to keep up with coursework, are seeking to better support all your students, or are looking to acquire new skills yourself, this book offers practical strategies you can tailor to your goals. It can also be a handy guide for advisory or homeroom periods, where you may have small amounts of time (between fifteen and forty-five minutes) you can use to guide students toward greater self-regulation for learning. You may also use the strategies in your classroom during instruction to help prepare students for post-secondary education and careers.

How to Use This Book

Drawing from research in educational psychology, neuroscience, and cognitive science, *Strategies and Tools for Self-Regulation in the Classroom* presents evidence-based strategies, tools, and techniques that are both effective and easy to implement. The book is made up of four parts that are structured around the four phases of learning, guiding you through fundamental concepts of self-regulation for each phase.

Each concept includes various strategies and tools you can incorporate into your practice and teach to students to help them build specific self-regulation skills and habits. And each section ends with an activity to help students practice the skills they're learning. Finally, the appendix offers several forms and graphic organizers students can use again and again throughout the learning process and the school year.

Here's what you'll find in each part.

PART I: FOSTERING CONFIDENCE FOR LEARNING

The initial phase of learning involves building and nurturing learner confidence. Confidence is a critical component of learning, as it motivates individuals to engage with materials and information and persist through challenges. Here's what's included in part I:

- **Attitude Counts.** Developing a positive outlook helps learners approach challenges with resilience and optimism, increasing their motivation and persistence.
- **Being On Time.** Timeliness goes beyond arriving to appointments or class at the scheduled hour. It includes prioritizing tasks and meeting deadlines, and it can reduce students' stress overall, leading to a more balanced and productive learning experience.

- **Learning Preferences.** Recognizing their individual learning preferences enables students to adopt strategies that suit them best, enhancing their comprehension and retention of information.
- **Get Organized.** Organizational skills help learners keep track of materials, assignments, and deadlines, fostering a more efficient and structured approach to their studies.
- **Health and Well-Being.** Maintaining physical and mental well-being through proper nutrition, exercise, and rest ensures that students have the energy and focus needed for effective learning.

PART II: SETTING AND MANAGING LEARNING GOALS

Once confidence is established, the next phase of learning involves setting clear and achievable goals. Goals provide direction and purpose, guiding learners' efforts and focus. Here's what's covered in part II:

- **Setting Learning Goals.** Knowing how to set and work toward well-defined goals helps learners focus on what they want to achieve.
- **Time Management.** Establishing clear parameters for study sessions and tasks helps students manage their time efficiently and avoid procrastination. This practice also helps maintain a balanced schedule, ensuring that students are allocating sufficient time for learning, rest, and other activities.
- **Overcoming Obstacles.** Anticipating and preparing for potential challenges in the learning journey helps students develop resilience and problem-solving skills. By identifying possible obstacles in advance, learners can devise strategies to overcome them, reducing stress and maintaining steady progress toward their goals. This proactive approach fosters a growth mindset and builds students' confidence in their abilities to overcome difficulties.

PART III: MONITORING AND ADJUSTING LEARNING TECHNIQUES

The third phase of learning involves actively monitoring progress and making necessary adjustments to ensure that learning goals are met. Because it is the most robust phase of learning, part III has the most tools and strategies of the four parts in this book. It includes the following:

- **Listening.** Being a good listener is crucial, as it allows a learner to fully understand and engage with the material being presented. Listening involves not just hearing information but truly comprehending it, which can lead to better retention and more meaningful discussions.
- **Note-Taking.** Taking effective notes is an essential part of the learning process. It helps students organize and consolidate information, making it easier to review and study later. Effective notes capture the key points and concepts, aiding memory and understanding.
- **Inquiry.** Asking effective questions is a powerful tool for clarifying doubts, deepening knowledge, and fostering critical thinking. Good questions encourage interaction and engagement, and they stimulate further exploration of subject matter.
- **Study Methods That Work.** Employing a variety of study techniques can address students' various learning preferences and keep the study process dynamic and interesting. It also enhances comprehension and retention.
- **Home Study, Not Homework.** It is vital that students continuously assess their understanding and progress to ensure that they're meeting their learning goals. This allows for timely adjustments to strategies and techniques, leading to more effective and efficient learning.

- **Technology.** Technology can greatly enhance the learning process by providing access to a wide range of resources, tools, and information. Effective use of technology also enables collaboration and communication with peers and teachers, further enriching the learning experience.

PART IV: REVIEWING AND REFLECTING ON LEARNING

The final phase consolidates learning and prepares learners for future endeavors. Part IV covers these topics:

- **Self-Assessment.** Regularly revisiting and summarizing learned material reinforces learners' retention and understanding.
- **Reflection.** Reflecting on the learning journey helps students identify what worked well, what could be improved, and how the strategies they used can be applied to future learning experiences.
- **Reward, Relax, Recharge.** Celebrating milestones and accomplishments, as well as relaxing and recharging for what comes next, helps students maintain motivation for learning and acknowledge their efforts.

SELF-REGULATION FOR ALL AGES

When determining which strategies and activities in this book to teach and use with your students, it is crucial to consider their age and developmental stage to ensure that the activities and ideas are engaging, appropriate, and effective. Younger and older students have different interests, abilities, and learning preferences, requiring tailored approaches to their educational experiences and to developing their SRL skills. For younger students, activities should focus on building fundamental SRL skills such as sharing, cooperation, communication, and mindfulness. Role-playing, storytelling, and group games can effectively teach these skills. For older students, self-regulation activities can be more sophisticated, including team-building exercises, leadership training, and peer mediation. These activities address the complex social dynamics, stressors, and emotional challenges adolescents face. Techniques such as journaling, meditation, and counseling sessions can be beneficial.

For all students, it is essential to focus on balancing the ABCs (Affect, Behavior, and Cognition) of SRL. This kind of self-reflection, whether undertaken by younger or older students, can have a powerful impact on their personal and academic development.

Conclusion

Strategies and Tools for Self-Regulation in the Classroom is your companion for guiding students to become more effective, independent, and resilient learners. By helping students master the art of self-regulation, you can help them unlock their full potential and achieve your teaching goals with confidence and ease.

I invite you to embark on this work equipped with the knowledge and tools to assist your students in taking control of their learning and thriving in an ever-changing world. Together, let's explore the possibilities and grow engaged, empowered, self-regulated learners.

PART I:
Fostering Confidence for Learning

Engagement and confidence are two fundamental psychological constructs that often intersect and influence each other. This intricate relationship can significantly impact students' performance, well-being, and overall success.

At its core, engagement is the ability to focus and resist distractions—a challenge in a world filled with distraction. Technology and media, emotional responses and physical needs, interaction and isolation—they all constantly compete for students' attention. And they all affect students' abilities to stay involved, committed, and enthusiastic about activities or tasks in the classroom.

Confidence is feeling sure of oneself and one's abilities and secure in what one can accomplish. It is not about arrogance or about feeling or being better than others. Confident learners are more likely to ask questions, seek help, acknowledge mistakes, take charge of their learning, set realistic goals, and put forth effort. In other words, confident learners are more likely to engage in learning.

Confidence is characteristic of self-regulated learners. And it is not limited to the affective dimension of SRL. Confident learners know the value of hard work and of putting effort into building their skills. They also must keep in check their internal dialogue and sense of self-belief to build self-efficacy, or trust in themselves to analyze their performance and make necessary adjustments.

The strategies in this section can assist you in developing confident, engaged, and self-regulated learners who are ready to take ownership of their learning.

Attitude Counts

Psychologically, the term *attitude* refers to "a set of emotions, beliefs, and behaviors toward a particular object, person, thing, or event. Attitude can also be described as the way we evaluate something or someone" (Cherry 2024). The three dimensions of self-regulation each have a substantial impact on a student's attitude toward learning. The cognitive dimension includes how students think about themselves—their self-beliefs—and their awareness of their abilities—their self-efficacy (cognition). Students' self-beliefs and self-efficacy are strongly related to the attitudes they have about a topic, subject, or learning environment (affect). And students' attitudes have significant impacts on what they do (behavior) and the general feelings they bear toward themselves and others.

Students' attitudes also direct their attention toward learning or away from learning. And their attitudes can be impacted by the level of confidence students feel in the classroom and in themselves as learners. You've likely seen this in action, and research backs it up: A positive attitude can have a significant influence on a child's academic learning and success (Chen et al. 2018). Therefore, it is important that students learn how to identify their attitudes and ways to shift them, when needed, to maintain confidence through learning challenges.

Strategies for Teachers

As a teacher, you are essential to the development of student attitudes and classroom culture! The strategies that follow help you build a classroom environment that promotes student confidence, intellectual risk-taking, and a positive attitude toward learning.

ENSURE THAT STUDENTS FEEL SAFE AND COMFORTABLE

One of the most effective ways to build and support positive student attitude and confidence toward learning is to ensure that students feel safe and comfortable in the learning space. This includes feeling safe from bullying, name-calling, and sarcasm; safe to take intellectual risks and be wrong without retribution; safe to work alone or with others; and safe to be themselves.

Here are a few ways to increase student comfort and safety. Also see pages 35–38 in *Self-Regulation in the Classroom: Helping Students Learn How to Learn* for more ideas.

- **Smile at your students and encourage them to smile at you!** Show a humorous clip from a movie, tell a funny story or joke, show a single-frame cartoon based on what's going on in class, and share good news.
- **Greet students as they enter the room.** When a student is late, rather than use punitive language ("Why are you late?"), welcome them in ("I'm so glad you're here.").
- **Routinely celebrate students' successes,** no matter how small.
- **Use humor, *not* sarcasm.** Since sarcasm is often used to belittle or put someone down, students may find sarcastic remarks hurtful, either to themselves or to others.
- **Allow students to choose where they sit,** within reason.
- **If you have space, provide different types of seats** (barstools, beanbags, pillows, carpet space, desks, tables).
- **Avoid harsh lighting** (natural light is best), loud sounds/noises, and strong smells/odors (this includes perfumes and colognes, scented lotions, and essential oils).

CREATE A PREDICTABLE ENVIRONMENT

You are a big part of the classroom environment, so be sure you are consistent in your mood. Try to stay even-keeled when you are having a bad day or are dealing with stress. Talk to your students about how you manage your stress in positive ways and how you maintain a positive attitude. Make sure to show students how you can laugh at yourself when you make a mistake. Other ways to create a predictable classroom environment include the following:

- posting timelines, schedules, and due dates
- posting lesson objectives and the "why" of the learning
- helping students adjust to changes and disruptions

CREATE POSITIVE NORMS AND EXPECTATIONS

You won't have an overall positive classroom atmosphere that supports positive attitudes toward learning if you're always telling students what they can't or shouldn't do. Start your classroom norms/expectations with "Do," keep them short and general rather than specific, and use simple language that is direct and to the point. Here are a few examples:

- Do support each other.
- Do be safe and respectful.
- Do follow directions.

Keep the number of norms/expectations to three to five. Be sure to review them with students routinely, using visuals or graphics to help students seal them into memory, and expect that students be able to recite the classroom norms when asked. You can also post your norms/expectations, along with any supporting graphics, as a visual reminder. Apply your classroom norms consistently, and offer support or guidance as needed to help students follow the norms.

USE AFFIRMATIONS

Affirmations are an easy tool you can use to support an overall positive atmosphere and boost student confidence in your classroom. Here are a few ideas for how to incorporate affirmations into your daily practice:

- **Create an affirmations wall in your space and fill it with positive phrases.** Students can look at the wall and pick a positive phrase they'll say to themselves throughout the class period, day, or week.
- **Write affirmations on sticky notes and stick them around the external frame of your classroom door.** Ask students to take one as they enter the room. They can post their chosen affirmations on their desks as a reminder of the kind messages they'd like to tell themselves. Students then create their own affirmations to replace the ones they take from the doorframe. This way you never run out of positive messages.
- **Have students work in teams to create alphabet books of positive affirmations.** The more creative they get, the better. Here are a few examples. I am/we are:
  - **A:** amazing, awesome, astounding
  - **B:** beautiful, breathtaking, brilliant
  - **C:** caring, creative, cheerful
  - **D:** dynamic, determined, diligent

Also, be sure to mix up your affirmations. So often, we get stuck using a few phrases repeatedly. This repetition can start to ring hollow or feel inauthentic to students. Instead, try to use a variety of affirming messages to lighten the mood in your classroom.

USE ENCOURAGING LANGUAGE

Using encouraging language is another way to help students keep a positive attitude. As with affirmations, try to use a variety of encouraging statements to help students feel individually important. Here are twenty phrases you might incorporate into your interactions with students.

20 Affirming Statements of Encouragement

1. I believe in you!
2. You've got this.
3. We are all in this together.
4. I'm here to help you, guide you, and ensure your success.
5. I'm here to support you.
6. I'm grateful to have you in my class.
7. I'm lucky you are sharing your thoughts.
8. You are a hard worker, and it is paying off.
9. You can always count on me to be in your corner.
10. You are doing great things.
11. Your effort is what is going to make you successful.
12. I recognize your talent.
13. Keep working at it. You will get it.
14. You may have failed, but that doesn't mean you are a failure.
15. Mistakes are part of the learning process. What will you do differently next time?
16. Never be afraid to ask questions.
17. Hang in there. Tomorrow is a new day.
18. Don't give up! You've got this.
19. Trust yourself and keep going. Worrying about the outcome won't change it.
20. Breathe!

INVITE SHOUT-OUTS

Near the end of a period or day, encourage students to recognize a peer or peers who represented positivity or were helpful to others' learning. Share an example or two to get the group started:

- "I want to recognize Nico for being helpful to me during the lesson."
- "A shout-out to Mariko for always being a positive influence."
- "Here's to Bobbi, who has shown me how to work hard."
- "Thank you, Amalia, Sean, and Araby, for being great teammates."
- "Cheers to Corey and Monica for their accomplishments this week."

Acknowledging others and being acknowledged in a public way supports students' positive attitudes and individual confidence. Celebrating the help students offer one another and the effort they put forth toward learning also promotes the value of being in a learning community.

BUILD IN BRAIN BREAKS

The brain learns information best when allowed time to process and connect new ideas. To support an overall positive classroom atmosphere, try to adhere to the 10:2/20:2 rule. This rule reflects the amount of information the brain can handle before it needs to download or use that information.

- **For students who need more support, use the 10:2 model.** For every ten minutes of instruction, allow up to two minutes for discussion, application, movement, or restating what was learned.
- **For students who are more self-regulated, use the 20:2 model.** For every twenty minutes of instruction, allow up to two minutes for discussion, application, movement, or restating what was learned.

Techniques and Tools for Students

Attitude matters! And students' attitudes have a tremendous influence on many areas of their lives. Share these tools and techniques to help students build confidence and maintain a positive attitude.

ADDRESS NEGATIVE THOUGHTS

One way students can maintain confidence and a positive attitude is to talk back to thoughts that aren't so positive. Teach students to sit quietly and listen to their self-talk before class and periodically throughout a lesson. Is it positive or negative? If a student's self-talk is negative, they can recite an affirmation silently.

Instruct students that when negative self-talk begins, they should pause and try to identify what may be causing the negative talk. Here are a number of factors to consider:

- the environment, such as room temperature, smells, harsh lighting, or sounds ("It's too noisy in here.")
- people or social interactions ("Kaeleigh bothers me when we work together.")
- content ability or interest ("I'm bad at math/math is boring.")
- past events ("Last time I failed, so I'll probably fail again.")
- future worries ("If I don't get an A, my parents will be mad.")
- the teacher ("Ms. Johnson doesn't like me.")
- distractors, such as smartphones or other external distractions ("I need my phone or else I won't know what's happening with my friends.")
- lack of reward or influence of expected/perceived punishment ("What do I need to get an A?")
- comparison to others ("Jibril always gets to be first.")
- behaviors of others ("My brother is so annoying!")

After students have identified negative thoughts, it's time to challenge and address them. Teach these techniques.

Challenge Negative Thoughts

One of the easiest ways to do this is to ask these three questions:

1. Is the thought true?
2. Is the thought helpful?
3. Is the thought real?

Often, the answer to these questions is no, but negative thoughts can be connected to real worries a student has. When negative thoughts are connected to worries, remind students that though their worries may be very real, worrying cannot change the eventual outcome.

The Power of Yet

This is an easy tool to teach, and even easier for students to use. All students have to do is add the word *yet* to the end of their negative thoughts. The Power of Yet can help students understand that many of the obstacles in their lives are temporary. And approaching hurdles with a positive attitude shows that they are willing to try.

- I can't do this . . . yet.
- I don't like this . . . yet.
- I'm not good at this . . . yet.

USE AFFIRMATIONS

Teach students how to build their own positive and affirming self-talk. Share the list of positive affirmations on page 119 and ask students to choose three to five affirmations that they'll say to themselves every day. They can also create their own affirmations to add to the list. Discuss times when they will use their affirmations. Will they say them every morning? Before bed? Write them on an index card or sticky note that they carry with them? Talk about the importance of returning to affirmations in moments of struggle and self-doubt, when experiencing negative self-talk, or when confidence slips.

50 Affirmations to Try

1. I can do this.
2. I am confident in myself.
3. I am proud of who I've become.
4. I have the right to be happy.
5. I am powerful.
6. I am strong.
7. I get better each time I try.
8. I am an unstoppable force.
9. I inspire others to do better.
10. I may fail, but I learn each time.
11. I haven't done XYZ yet, but eventually I will.
12. My attitude is contagious. I hope others catch my good vibes.
13. My joy/happiness is worth passing along to others.
14. I work hard to achieve success.
15. I will stay focused on my success.
16. I've overcome obstacles in the past. I can do it this time too.
17. My hard work will show in my achievements.
18. Each day, I get better and better.
19. I believe in myself.
20. I can do almost anything I put my mind to.
21. I am freeing myself from negative thoughts.
22. I accept who I am, and I will continue to do great things.
23. I deserve to be happy/successful.
24. I have made mistakes, but they don't define me.
25. I like myself the way I am.
26. I choose happiness.
27. Struggles make me stronger.
28. I am a strong and capable person.
29. It may be hard, but it's worth the challenge.
30. I am allowed to be sad, mad, or unhappy. It's part of being human.
31. I am allowed to be happy.
32. I can set boundaries without feeling bad about it.
33. I am worthy of praise and support.
34. The past is the past. Today is a new beginning.
35. I matter.
36. Growth can be difficult, but I'm getting better every day.
37. When I get stressed, I can remember to breathe.
38. I'm not bored. I'm waiting for inspiration.
39. I will avoid distractions during XYZ.
40. I work hard to be my best self.
41. Even though I may not win, I will do my best.
42. My feelings are mine. I will remain positive through difficult feelings.
43. Each breath gives me peace/strength/power.
44. I live in the moment.
45. I am grateful for all the things I have.
46. I am filled with joy.
47. I greet challenges with gratitude.
48. Today, I choose to be happy.
49. I embrace my uniqueness, because there is no one like me!
50. I can do hard things.

119

MORE ATTITUDE BOOSTERS

Share these attitude-boosting tips with students and incorporate them into your teaching practice.

- Make sure to laugh every day.
- Focus on goals.
- Surround yourself with positive people.
- Listen to music that makes you happy.
- Practice yoga or mindfulness.
- Breathe! Take in a deep breath through the nose, hold it for three seconds, and exhale out through the mouth to release stress, anxiety, fear—and negative thoughts. Repeat as many times as needed.

CREATIVE DRAMATICS

Creative dramatics are wonderful activities to do at the beginning of a school year or quarter, or whenever you have a new group of students come together. These collaborative and playful games help students become comfortable with one another, learn to respect personal space, and learn peers' names—all of which have a positive impact on their attitudes and confidence in the classroom. All students should participate in creative dramatics to the best of their abilities. Students with physical limitations move as they can—no child should be excluded due to any limitation.

If a student is unwilling or unable to participate by following directions, ask them to watch the game from the sidelines. Have the student observe the rest of the group, citing the ways their peers demonstrated the skills being practiced in the activity or contributed to the success of the group.

Creative dramatics can be used during advisory periods or in that last bit of time at the end of class. You can also incorporate content connections. Some examples include having students walk as if they're a character from a book (language arts) or in particular shapes (math) during a Space Walk activity; inviting them to create new legislation (social studies) or hybrid organisms (science) during an Ad Game; or switching up the cards or categories in a ROLE game (for example, use ROBE—reaction, outcome, bond, element—categories in science).

SPACE WALK

In this game, students must work together to move around each other in space and to start and stop as one.

Process:

1. Define a "space" that is clear of obstruction and barriers. Show students the boundaries of the space—students must stay within the boundaries while playing the game.
2. Ask students to come to the space and walk without making any sounds. (You might do this with the full group or a small group, depending on the size of your space.) Students are to pay attention to others in the space, avoid bumping into each other, and stay aware of the group.
3. Inform the group that they are to stop as one when you say "STOP." They start walking again when you say "START."
4. Repeat the start and stop as many times as necessary until the group can stop as one.

Other considerations: To switch things up, have students try different types of walking, such as walking in pudding, walking with purpose, walking to the principal's office, or walking to a favorite event. They might also try walking as if they're wearing different types of shoes, such as athletic shoes, high heels, sandals, a shoe with a broken heel, shoes that are too big/small, clown shoes, and so on. You might also consider having a student lead this activity while you watch the group and observe how students interact, how well they follow directions, and how well they can move as one.

SPACE WALK—GIVE AND TAKE

In this game, students communicate nonverbally as they pass or take movement from each other.

Process:

1. Begin this activity with the Space Walk. Have the group stop and assume a comfortable position.
2. **Give:** In Give, only one person may move at a time. The leader moves around the group, weaving in and out of the other group members. The leader stops and gives the movement over to another member. This student is the new leader. There is no need to verbally alert the new leader of the "give"—students should sense that they have been given the opportunity to move. This passing of movement continues until all members have had a chance to move. The activity is done in silence, until students are comfortable and understand the method.
3. **Take:** Now students do the opposite of Give. One person moves until another member "takes" the movement away. Again, no words or signals should be exchanged. Students must build a sense of community to "feel" when someone takes the movement away. If more than one student moves, call "STOP" to pause the members. Have them regroup, refocus, and retry.

Other considerations: Students not moving should watch for members who may not be giving or taking with fairness. Encourage students to use their whole bodies as they move, noting that they can walk tall, crouch, or even crawl.

AD GAME

In this game, you will ask students to SCAMPER a new product. SCAMPER is an acronym that was developed in the business community to help people come up with new ideas and think outside the box. You can use this technique to guide students to think more broadly about a topic, come up with unique products or projects, and make learning more fun. Here's what SCAMPER stands for: **Substitute, Combine, Adapt/adjust/add, Modify/minimize/maximize, Put to other use, Eliminate, Reverse/revise/rearrange.**

Process:

1. Put students in teams of five to eight.
2. Have each team SCAMPER an existing product or create something entirely new.
3. After students have SCAMPERed, tell them they will act as advertising teams to sell their new products. However, they may not confer with others on their team.
4. Students form a line with their team and randomly step forward to make a statement that describes the worthiness of their team's product. After the first person, each student begins their statement with "Yes, and . . ." to build on the prior statement.
5. Continue until all team members have had a chance to share a statement. Remember: There are no mistakes—only opportunities.

Other considerations: Begin by SCAMPERing common objects, such as a pencil or pen, to create new products until students are accustomed to the process. Encourage students to SCAMPER to solve problems in their daily lives.

THINK FAST!

In this game, students must pay attention and work together to complete rounds faster than other groups.

Process:

1. Collect an assortment of objects (such as a small empty container, a foot of plastic tubing, a wooden spoon) and place them in a large bag.
2. Arrange students in group of eight to ten. Have each group pull one object out of the bag.
3. Students pass the object around their group, with each person coming up with a new way to use the object or a new idea for what the object could be (other than what it really is). Students may not repeat what someone else has said, nor can they "pass." The group that can get the object around the circle the fastest "wins" the round.
4. Play as many rounds as desired.

Other considerations: Encourage students to use all their senses while doing this activity. For students who need more time to think, practice this activity without the pressure of speed—slowly building student confidence before attempting the speed challenge.

R.O.L.E.

Process:

1. Using four different colors of index cards, create four categories: **Role, Occasion, Location,** and **Emotion.** On the cards, write words that correspond to each of the categories. For example:
   - Role: mechanic, florist, patrol officer
   - Occasion: birthday, wedding, graduation
   - Location: at a lake, on a boat, in a park
   - Emotion: happy, sad, crabby

   You can also have teams create their own sets of ROLE cards.
2. Put students in small groups. Each group randomly selects one card from each category.
3. Each group must create a scene or develop a story that includes all four categories. Then each group presents their scene or story to the other groups.
4. At the end of each performance, students in the audience guess which four cards the performing group drew.

Other considerations: On the cards, use content vocabulary or words that may be unfamiliar to students—they can investigate the words and then use them within multiple contexts.

DR. KNOW-IT-ALL

In this activity, a small group of students must work together as "one mind" to be Dr. Know-It-All. This is a great activity for review or to prepare students for an upcoming quiz or exam.

Process:

1. Arrange five to eight chairs at the front of your space. Invite students to fill the seats. Tell them they are to act as the brain of Dr. Know-It-All to answer questions from the class.
2. Have a student ask Dr. Know-It-All a question. Alternatively, you might have students work collaboratively to come up with a question. The students acting as Dr. Know-It-All answer the question. However, each member may say only one word. When all members have spoken their one word, they should have answered the question.
3. If incorrect answers happen, it is up to students to ask follow-up questions to correct the misinformation. Remember: There are no mistakes—only opportunities.
4. Rotate the groups, making sure every student gets a chance to be a part of the mind of Dr. Know-It-All.

Other considerations: It's helpful if you or a student acts as a moderator during this activity. Then, when nonsensical or incorrect answers happen, the moderator can redirect the question for Dr. Know-It-All to try again. The moderator can also record the one-word responses on chart paper or the board to help the group make sense of Dr. Know-It-All's answers.

Being on Time

At most schools, there's a start and end time for the day and for classes. Being on time is a cultural expectation, and most teachers have had a student arrive late, causing the student to miss key information or you to restart your instruction. But being on time isn't just important in the classroom—it's a lifelong skill with benefits that will serve students far beyond their school years.

Punctuality is often regarded as a virtue that reflects a person's commitment, reliability, and respect for others. Whether for a class, a restaurant reservation, or a doctor's appointment, being on time shows consideration for everyone involved—whether that's a teacher, peers, service staff, or a doctor. In a connected world, knowing the time on the other side of the country or the globe is critical to an efficient work schedule.

The ability to be punctual can also significantly influence a person's confidence and overall well-being. Being on time helps reduce anxiety and stress. It also helps in maintaining relationships with friends, family, and colleagues by respecting others' time. It can even help a person save money by avoiding late fees and charges for rush orders.

Being on time can be difficult for students, since it requires planning. It can also be difficult because, until students can get themselves out the door and where they need to go without an adult, their ability to be on time for school is dependent on others. Timeliness can also be interrupted by technical challenges or difficulties translating time differences. However, students can still practice punctuality during the school day—ensuring they arrive on time to different classes, return from lunch on time, and keep track of their responsibilities and activities for the day and week. To be punctual, students need to learn how to plan and how to adjust their plan if something happens along the way.

In the classroom, punctuality is more than a mere habit; it is a fundamental characteristic of self-regulated learners, and it promotes a positive and productive learning environment. Being on time (behavior) enhances student focus (cognition) by ensuring that learners are engaging from the beginning of a task or activity and not missing out on important announcements or introductory information. In this way, punctuality can lead to better academic performance, which in turn will build students' confidence in learning by reducing stress and anxiety (affect). Punctuality demonstrates a person's level of discipline and time management. And it is a skill that students will use every day of their lives.

Strategies for Teachers

Though punctuality is most dependent upon students, teachers can still provide structures in the classroom to encourage student timeliness and show students how they keep themselves on track. Following are a few ideas for creating a positive learning environment that teaches students the power of punctuality. For more strategies on setting and managing time, see the section on time management in part II (page 51).

POST SCHEDULES AND TIMELINES

Share your schedule for the day in a location where students can easily see it. As you move through the day, try to highlight what's to come or when the next period/subject begins.

You can also post your timeline for each class period, including how long you'll spend on each part of the lesson. For example:

- 9:00–9:05 Introduction of the objectives for the lesson (5 minutes)
- 9:15–9:30 Mini-lesson on the skill to be developed (15 minutes)
- 9:30–9:32 Organize into small working groups (2 minutes)

- 9:32–9:47 Small working group time (15 minutes)
- 9:47–9:57 Wrap up and set the agenda for the next day (10 minutes)
- 9:57–10:00 Reflection and reward (3 minutes)

Refer to the timeline as you move through your lessons. When you get off track or something takes longer than planned, talk about how you will adjust to get back on schedule.

STICK TO THE SCHEDULE

There will always be the occasional fire drill or disruptive announcement to contend with when teaching. Those events are beyond your control. However, when you are in control, make sure to adhere to your schedule as closely as possible, as often as you can. If you want students to be on time, you must be on time too. You can also show students how you work your schedule around planned events like pep rallies and field trips—and how you ensure that the class shows up on time for them.

Techniques and Tools for Students

The following techniques and tools can help students stay on time and increase their productivity, happiness, and social connections. For more on helping students set and manage their time, see the section on time management in part II (page 51).

FIGURE OUT WHAT NEEDS TO CHANGE

Some students are chronically late. They may be prone to anxiety or highly distractable or they might be perfectionists, procrastinators, or just poor planners. Or they may be late due to forces beyond their control. To avoid tardiness as a habit, focus on timeliness where students have some degree of control. Help them figure out what may be the root cause of their tardiness in these situations, then work from there.

CREATE AND FOLLOW A SCHEDULE

Setting and maintaining a schedule can improve a student's academic performance by helping them adjust how they use their time each day. Following a schedule can also help students reduce stress, increase organization, and take charge of their learning. To help them learn to create and use schedules, try the following ideas.

Set a Schedule

To teach the skill of setting a schedule, first show students how to break their activities and responsibilities into the following categories:

- Academic time (this includes their class schedule, how much time they need for studying, and how many projects/assignments they have)
- Extracurricular activities (this includes their activities and work before, during, and after school)
- Self-care time (this includes when they wind down, go to bed, and wake up; how much time they spend exercising; and mealtimes)
- Social time (this includes the time they spend socializing with family and friends)
- Personal time (this includes time for activities, hobbies, responsibilities at home, and errands)

After students have categorized their time, it's time to put everything on their calendars. Students may use electronic calendars or scheduling apps, paper calendars, or a combination of both.

- **Electronic calendars.** Some students, and especially older students, may prefer to use their personal devices for scheduling. There are many software applications available. You can help them choose one that fits their lifestyle, learning preferences, and budget. They can install it on their device or laptop—and you can show them how to add notifications so the app can help them stay on track. Let students know that while it can be annoying at first to have an app inform them about every move they need to make, in time they may come to appreciate the convenience of being on time and working efficiently. If they try an electronic schedule for a few weeks and it's not working for them, they should try a different one. And there's always the option to use a physical calendar or planner instead.
- **Physical calendars.** Many people like to have a paper calendar instead of, or in addition to, an electronic one. Using a paper calendar or planner is an important strategy for younger students, who often don't have access to personal electronic devices. Two examples of paper calendars—daily and weekly—are included on pages 120 and 121. Have students practice using different types of physical calendars to find the one that best fits their needs or work habits.

When they're beginning to use schedules, encourage students to try the following tips:

- **Keep the schedule as simple as possible.** Being too elaborate and posting too many things into the schedule may make it seem daunting and overwhelming.
- **Break down the schedule into three parts of the day:** before school, during school, and after school.
- **Once a simplified schedule is mastered, work in the five categories** (listed above) to make the schedule more comprehensive.
- **In general, try to plan more time than expected in the schedule.** This can help when hurdles or other things come up, and it can reduce stress. And when hurdles don't pop up and a project is completed before it's due, celebrate by inserting some fun or relaxation into the day.

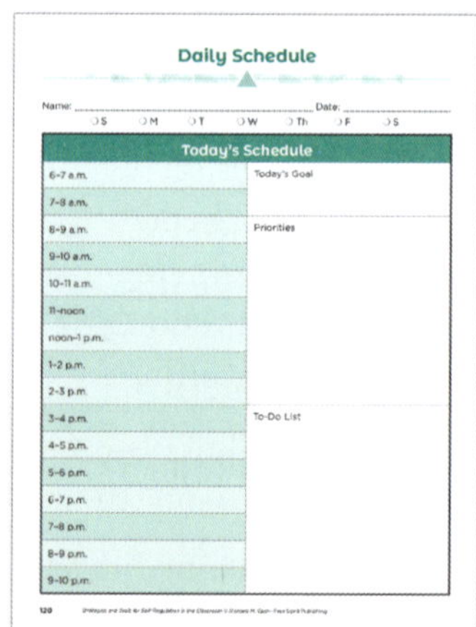

Monitor the Schedule

While it's important that students follow their schedules, it's also important that they monitor them and allow for flexibility. Remind students not to let the schedule control them. Rather, it's there to inform, guide, and ensure that they are planful and have routines. Using timers and tracking work time are two ways students can monitor their schedules.

Timers can help students plan their time, pace their work, and transition from one activity to another. The use of timers while learning can also help students focus their attention, predict how much work needs to happen within a set time, and manage stressful situations.

A great way to get students accustomed to using timers is to incorporate them into instruction. Some students may enjoy visual timers (like a kitchen timer), while some may like timers that show minutes and seconds counting down. Use various kinds of timers in your instruction to expose students to different types.

Timers can also be used to take efficient breaks. Breaks during learning are essential to maintaining focus and attention. During challenging activities, students may go off task easily. Setting timers so they know when they can take a break can help them stay focused until break time. Setting timers for the break itself can help students more easily transition back into work time when it ends.

As students move through their schedules, it's a good practice for them to track their time. They can note how much time it takes to complete each task or assignment. Was it more or less time than they'd originally allotted? (It can be especially helpful to use a timer for this kind of tracking.) Knowing how much time certain tasks took can be useful in setting the schedule next time. And knowing how much time they have and how much time they need may help students manage their time and schedule their days more efficiently. They may find that they have extra time to sleep in, hang out with friends, or relax.

Tracking work time can also make it clear to students when they are running behind or will not meet a due date. When they know they're running behind, they can adjust. Offer these ideas:

- Negotiate with the teacher for more time or a pared-down assignment.
- Prioritize the aspects of the project (see pages 34–35 for tips on prioritizing tasks) and complete what is essential.
- Submit quality partial work to show where they are headed for the final product.

Review Old Schedules

Part of creating and following a schedule is reviewing old schedules (from the past week or month) to identify what didn't work and make adjustments for the future. You can assist students in noting in their schedules where and when there was a need for more time or when things got in the way. Part of this involves looking back at when they didn't meet a due date or ran out of time. In reviewing such past mistakes, encourage students to be good to themselves and try not to worry too much about what's already happened. The experience is a learning opportunity. It's also important to note when challenges were met, things got in on time, and accomplishments happened—and then celebrate. Reflecting on their time in learning can help students do better next time!

Sometimes students (and adults) get in over their heads by saying yes too often. When students review their schedules, encourage them to look for times when they may have overscheduled or overcommitted. Help them find the "sweet spot" in their calendars—when their planning was just right. Students should realize they may sometimes need to say no to things that they really want to do or that are last-minute requests if these tasks could interfere with what needs to get done. Make sure students know that "others' poor planning is not my emergency." Saying no can free them of the stress of being overbooked and can even feel good when the load is lightened.

BE PREPARED

Another piece of punctuality is learning how to be prepared, present, and in the moment. Teach students to focus on what is important, especially in the classroom. They can learn to be ready with their notes, materials, and mindset, since some teachers or speakers may not give them the brain warm-up they need.

Especially in the older grades, it's up to students to be ready to learn and not wait for others to get them ready. You can also remind students to have a book, game, or some other item (whether physical or virtual) on hand to help them pass the time while waiting for others.

PUTTING THE STORY TOGETHER

In today's educational environment, fostering cooperation and critical thinking in students is essential. This activity combines these aspects into an engaging and interactive task. By reconstructing a paragraph from shuffled sentences, students not only practice their comprehension skills but also enhance their ability to work collaboratively under time constraints.

Preparation: Select a paragraph from a textbook or a work of literature. Print each sentence from the paragraph onto a small strip of paper. Place the strips of paper in a small bag—in a random order. Make enough bags for the number of groups you will have.

Process:

1. Organize students into small groups of five to seven.
2. Distribute the bags with the sentence strips.
3. Tell groups they will have ten minutes to put the strips of paper back together into a coherent paragraph. They will not be able to talk to each other during the ten minutes they are working together to re-create the paragraph.
4. At the end of the ten minutes, stop the groups and discuss the activity:
   - What was easy about this task?
   - What was difficult about it?
   - Was time a factor in your process?
   - How did manage your time?
   - What would you do to manage your time better?
   - How could this activity have been made easier?
   - What else did this activity teach you about? (Students may identify teamwork, knowing the context, or organization, for example.)

Learning Preferences

Much has been said and written about learning styles. While recent research has found little evidence that learning styles actually have any effect on learning, teachers must take these studies with a bit of salt (or sugar). The truth is that everyone has the capability to learn in a variety of ways. So rather than teaching students about learning *styles*, let's start talking about learning *preferences*.

Just as all people have different preferences and tastes when it comes to food, style, books, and movies, so too do they have preferred ways of doing and learning. Some prefer to do things in a step-by-step manner while others prefer to find their own way through a process. Some people choose to watch a YouTube video to learn how to repair their coffee maker, while others would rather read the owner's manual. None of these approaches is wrong or better than others. The key is getting the job done or completing the action successfully. So, don't think of learning preferences as a strict rule. Instead, consider them a guide to help students do better, no matter the style of teaching or the coursework.

Being able to identify how they prefer to learn (cognition) allows students to tailor their study habits, select classes or courses that fit their preferences and interests, and better prepare themselves for when classes or courses don't fit their preferences (behavior). It can help them find school more enjoyable, identify types of projects where they may find success, reduce inattentiveness, make learning difficult material less challenging, and even assist in thinking through future career or entrepreneurial options. When students know how they want to learn, they feel more confident taking on challenging tasks (affect). In other words, this knowledge helps them become self-regulated learners.

Additionally, when students know their preferred ways of learning and doing, they will also recognize that they need to put in additional effort when their preferred way of learning is not an option. If a student is a highly creative type, for example, learning mathematics in the sequential fashion may not come easy for them, but they also may not have the option to do it their way. Being flexible and knowing that sometimes they are going to have to work harder are critical skills for students' success in school and in the future.

Strategies for Teachers

In this section, three learning-type models are presented along with tools for teaching and identifying different learning types. There are also numerous learning-type models on the internet. It is best to select one or two that have some research or evidence behind them when sharing these ideas with students. As you read about each model presented here, think about yourself and the learners in your class. Ask:

- Which learning type(s) are you?
- Which learning types are present in your class?
- How might you adapt your lessons and activities to include the preferences of all learning types?

FOUR TYPES OF LEARNERS

Adapting from the work of Silver, Jackson, and Moirao (2011), I have found that there are four types of learners in every classroom: paper clips, teddy bears, magnifying glasses, and slinkies. While every student is a combination of all four types, students often have preferences in the way they like to work and produce. Recognizing that all students need to be competent in all the types, you should be sure to develop activities that address the four types as well as teach students how to shift between preferred and nonpreferred ways of learning and doing. This ability to adapt to different learning strategies is a powerful skill for future success. For more information on the Four Types of Learners, see pages 144–146 in *Self-Regulation in the Classroom: Helping Students Learn How to Learn.*

Figure 1: Four Types of Learners

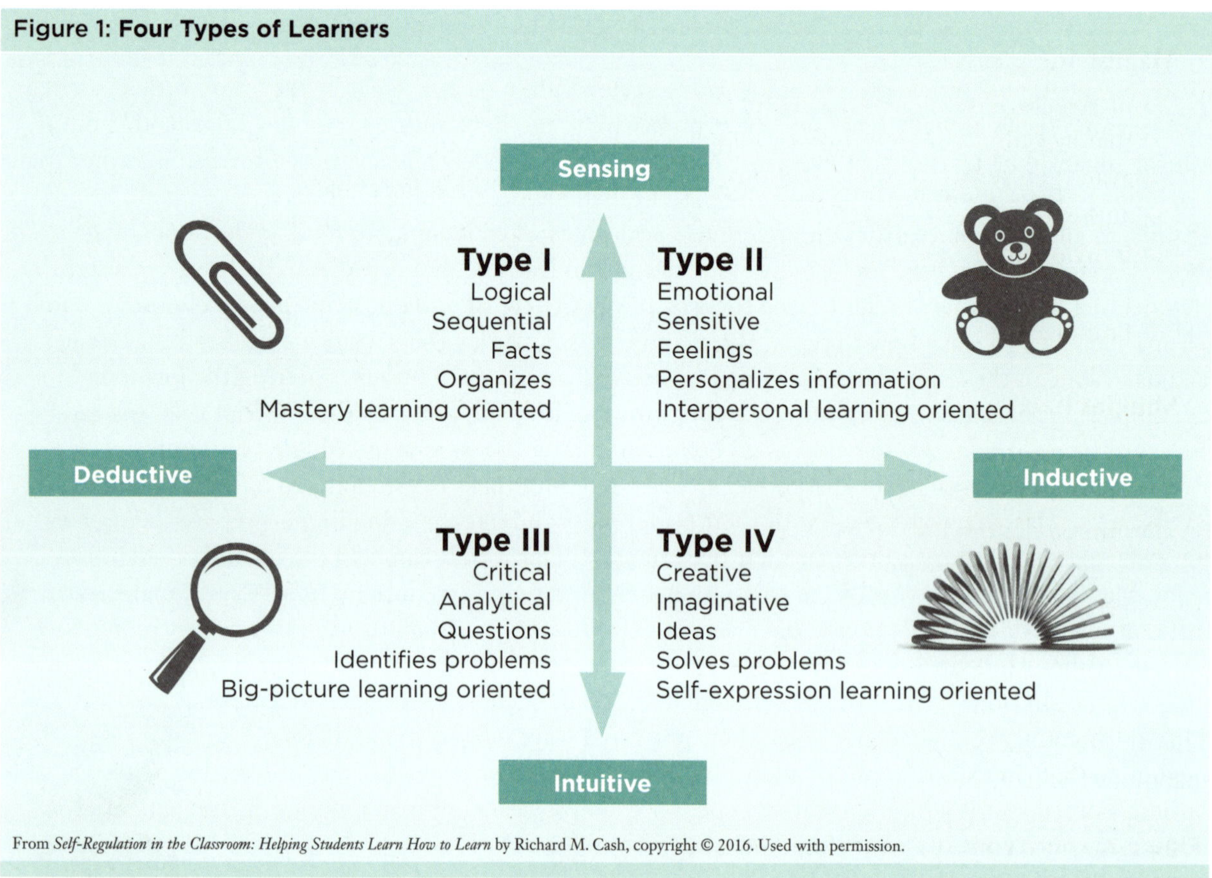

From *Self-Regulation in the Classroom: Helping Students Learn How to Learn* by Richard M. Cash, copyright © 2016. Used with permission.

You can use the Four Types of Learners to differentiate your learning activities. When students are aware of their preferred way of learning and doing, they can make better choices when provided options. It is also helpful for them to learn in a nonpreferred way sometimes. This will prepare them for the complexities of life and help them learn how to learn when options are limited. When constructing activities for the different types of learners, keep the following in mind.

Differentiating for the Four Types

Paper clips like:

- structured activities
- rules, regulations, rubrics to follow
- ordered ways of performing
- outlines in linear fashion
- step-by-step instructions

Paper clips need support with:

- open-ended activities
- disorganization
- few rules, regulations, or directions
- random tasks
- interruptions

Teddy bears like:

- partner work
- emotional engagement
- personal connections to the content
- human factors in context
- social justice perspectives

Teddy bears need support with:

- individualized tasks
- debating points of view
- straightforward directions
- dealing with adversity
- working through inauthentic (unreal) activities

Magnifying glasses like:	**Magnifying glasses need support with:**
› ill-structure problems (those problems that lack all the information or don't avail themselves to quick solutions) › authentic/real issues › individualized work logic/mysteries › puzzles › brain teasers	› understanding emotional reactions › listening to others' ideas › working in groups › making group decisions › working through problems where quick responses are required
Slinkies like:	**Slinkies need support with:**
› to be creative › open-ended activities › limited directions › active/physical involvement › group work	› waiting for their turns › listening to others › rules and regulations › taking time to think › meeting deadlines

Figure 2 shares how you might differentiate for each learning type in a group activity in geometry. This arrangement is a sequence of activities. In leading students through this activity, the teacher can encourage students of different learning types to take charge of different steps in the sequence.

Figure 2: Four Types of Learners—Geometry Example

Step 1: Paperclips
List the steps to remove the minimum number of pennies so that no three pennies lie on the vertices of an equilateral triangle. Be sure to be clear and precise.

Step 2: Teddy bears
After you have solved the puzzle, how does solving a problem like this prepare you for a real event?

Step 3: Magnifying glasses
Why do you think geometry is or is not an essential tool for your future?

Step 4: Slinkies
Using what you have learned in geometry, where else can you find it being applied? Think broadly and creatively.

STERNBERG'S SUCCESSFUL INTELLIGENCE

Dr. Robert Sternberg, one of the world's leading cognitive psychologists, has theorized a balance of intellectual abilities that he calls "successful intelligence." According to Sternberg, when people are aware of their strengths and abilities, they are more likely to use those strengths to compensate for or correct their limitations (Sternberg and Grigorenko 2007). And when people are able to use their strengths in effective ways, they are more likely to be successful in life. Successful individuals have figured out how to adapt to their environments, shape them, or choose environments where their abilities and strengths are best used.

Sternberg's design of successful intelligence has three ability dimensions: creative, analytical, and practical. While all people have each of these dimensions, they have varying degrees of ability in them. Helping students identify their own balances can assist them in understanding their learning preferences and selecting activities and study strategies that suit those preferences.

To teach this concept to students, show them a graphic like the one in figure 3 below. Invite them to identify people in their lives who may represent the various types of abilities, then have them define themselves as learners within the framework. Using this scaling technique can help students identify their strengths and where they may need support.

Figure 3: Sternberg's Successful Intelligence Scale

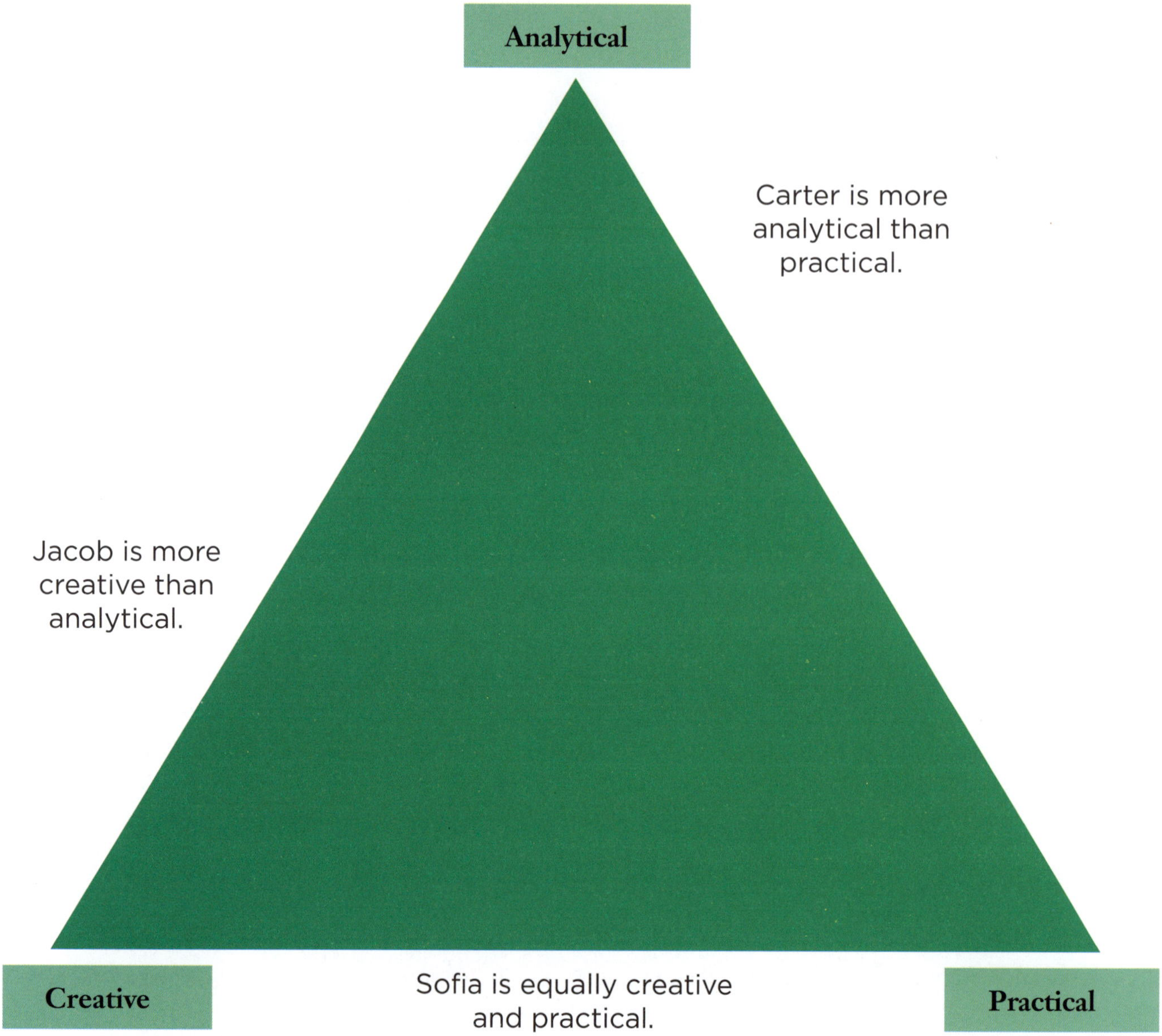

When constructing activities for the different types of learners, keep the following in mind.

Differentiating with Sternberg's Successful Intelligence

Creative people like:

- open-ended activities
- generating new and interesting ideas
- abstract thinking and connections
- coming up with new/novel ways to represent information
- inventing

Creative people need support with:

- standardized testing
- abiding by rules and structure
- closed-ended activities/one way to do something
- working on a timeline
- working alone

Analytical people like:

- rules, structure, and order
- standardized tests
- problem-solving
- step-by-step activities
- finding flaws in thoughts and reasoning

Analytical people need support with:

- open-ended activities
- lack of organization and structures
- disruptions
- working in groups
- abstract ideas

Practical people like:

- hands-on activities
- common sense
- authentic problems
- coming up with real solutions
- social interactions

Practical people need support with:

- working alone
- inauthentic problems with one right answer
- novelty
- theory and abstractions
- lecture

Figure 4 shares how you might differentiate for each learning type in language arts. An arrangement such as this might be used for developing a portfolio of assessements on a topic. Students would choose to do two to three of the types. You can use the keywords on page 26 as you craft differentiated learning activities for each learning type.

Figure 4: **Sternberg's Successful Intelligence—Language Arts Example**

FAKE NEWS INVASION

CREATIVE	ANALYTICAL	PRACTICAL
Choose 1: › Write your own fake news article using at least two techniques we learned. › Design a poster that warns viewers about fake news and how to identify it. › Film a PSA warning viewers about the dangers of fake news.	**Choose 1:** › Find an example of fake news and illustrate how it works. › Write an article or essay explaining how fake news works. › Describe the historical development of the fake news phenomenon.	**Choose 1:** › Write an article that describes the damage fake news does to society. › Send a response of some sort to a fake news perpetrator, explaining your objections. › Devise a policy that might help our society reduce or regulate fake news.

From the work of David Michael Slater, author and retired middle school teacher for the gifted and talented. Used with permission.

Keywords for Sternberg's Successful Intelligence

Creative	Analytical	Practical
Create	Analyze	Apply
Invent	Evaluate	Use
Discover	Judge	Implement
Connect	Critique	Collaborate
Explore	Compare/contrast	Work with tools
Imagine	Test	Operate
Pretend	Examine	Manipulate
Hypothesize	Study	Manage
Postulate	Investigate	Practice
Theorize	Question	Authenticate
Design	Organize	Make real

From Advancing Differentiation: Thinking and Learning for the 21st Century by Richard M. Cash, copyright © 2017. Used with permission.

V.A.T.K.

Another aspect of students' learning preferences is how they prefer to process information. The VATK (Visual, Auditory, Textual, Kinesthetic) learning styles can be helpful in guiding students to think about their information-processing preferences. This typology has a long history and somewhat unknown origin (Fallace 2023), and it's not without controversy.

Still, no person uses only one way of processing information exclusively. Therefore, it is important for students to be aware of the many different ways of gathering and processing information so they can be more efficient and confident in learning. When guiding students to identify how they prefer to process information, keep the following in mind.

Identifying VATK Processing Preferences

Students who have a visual learning preference may like:

- looking at images and graphics
- highlighting text to aid in memorization
- exploring maps, tables and charts
- viewing complex ideas in picture form
- watching videos about new information

Students who have an auditory learning preference may like:

- listening to audio books
- engaging in lectures and discussions
- using storytelling and the spoken word
- discussing complex issues and ideas to aid in understanding
- thinking out loud, either to themselves or others

Students who have a textual learning preference may like:

- reading about new ideas
- taking detailed notes during class
- summarizing complex ideas in their own words to aid in understanding
- describing charts and graphics in written form
- writing essays, poems, or scripts

Students who have a kinesthetic learning preference may like:

- learning by doing
- getting physical with information
- exploring and making models and artifacts that can be touched
- acting out or using their bodies to explain complex ideas
- using real-world/authentic applications of what they're learning

Techniques and Tools for Students

Knowing their learning types and preferences helps students understand themselves as learners and feel more confident in learning. Share these ideas for understanding their learning types and advocating for their learning needs.

IDENTIFY LEARNING PREFERENCES

One of the best ways to help students identify their learning types and preferences is to have them take learning surveys. Students can take the survey on page 122 a couple of times throughout the school year to determine which combination of the four learning types they are. You could also guide them through identifying where they fall on the sides of the triangle in Sternberg's model or share the table about VATK preferences above, inviting students to identify their own preferences from the list.

Periodically, students should meet with other like-minded learners and meet with a cross-section of different types of learners. When students meet, provide these questions for discussion:

- How are we alike?
- How are we different?
- How might we support each other when things become difficult?
- What is the strength of being this kind of learner?
- When will we need to seek the help of others?

Student Learning Survey

Name: ______________ Date: ______________

Check all the statements that are true for you.

Paper Clip

- ☐ I like to have a timeline for doing work.
- ☐ I am most comfortable doing things by myself.
- ☐ I like to keep myself organized.
- ☐ I feel best when I accomplish a task completely
- ☐ I like to make lists of what needs to be done.
- ☐ I believe it is important to follow rules and directions.
- ☐ I feel frustrated when I don't know the right answer.
- ☐ I like to do things that are step-by-step.
- ☐ I work best when I know what is expected.

If you agree with a majority of these statements, you may be considered a "paper clip" type of learner.

As a paper clip, you feel comfortable with:

- schedules and deadlines
- knowing what is going to happen and when it will happen
- organization
- step-by-step directions

As a paper clip, you may need support with:

- dealing with changes to the schedule
- not knowing what is coming next
- disorganization
- random tasks

122

CREATE A PERSONAL LEARNING PLAN

A personal learning plan is a student-centered approach that empowers a learner to take control of their educational journey. It is a structured plan that outlines a student's goals, strategies, hurdles, and progress. One of the most compelling benefits of a personal learning plan is that it can be tailored to accommodate the unique strengths, preferences, and goals of an individual. By recognizing and integrating students' learning preferences, these plans enhance students' self-efficacy and their enjoyment of the learning process. See page 126 for a form students can use as they create their own learning plans.

Figure 5: Personal Learning Plan Example

Who do I want to be?
I would like to be a thoughtful leader who inspires others to do well in whatever they choose to do.

How does this class help?
I may not be the best at geometry, so I know I will learn how to persevere when things get tough—this can help me understand when others have difficulties.

What do I need to do?
Work hard and keep my focus on doing my best.

What are the hurdles?
Time to study will be difficult for me, because I have to work after school and sometimes babysit my little sister.

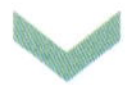

How will I overcome those hurdles?
Make sure to plan time either on the weekends or on my days off work to get my school work done.

Who is my goal buddy?	**Goal buddy's signature**
Marcella Simmons	*Marcella Simmons*

Created by Katharine McCoy, math teacher, Bishop DuBourg HS, St. Louis, MO. Used with permission.

USE TECHNOLOGY AND DIGITAL TOOLS

Technology and digital tools enhance learning experiences by making them more interactive and engaging. Digital tools such as educational games, virtual reality (VR), and augmented reality (AR) can bring subjects to life, capturing students' attention and making learning fun. These tools can also facilitate experiential learning, allowing students to explore and interact with content in ways that are not possible with traditional methods.

Technology can be used to enhance collaboration through video conferencing, Google Docs, and other virtual learning platforms. It can also increase accessibility for learners who need more direct support. Assistive technology features such as text-to-speech, speech-to-text, and closed captioning can support students with disabilities, while translation tools can assist multilingual students.

Artificial intelligence (AI) has revolutionized numerous industries, and education is no exception. Students today have an unprecedented opportunity to leverage AI tools to enhance their learning experience, tackle complex problems, and achieve academic success. AI can personalize learning, create adaptive activities by adjusting levels of text or content complexity, and provide tutoring opportunities, to name a few. See the section on technology in part III (page 97) for more on the use of AI in the classroom.

ADVOCATE FOR LEARNING NEEDS

Self-advocacy is the ability to understand and communicate one's needs and desires. Self-advocacy in learning involves students taking responsibility for their education, seeking help when necessary, and making informed decisions about their learning. By being empowered to take charge of their own learning, students can achieve greater academic success and personal growth.

To effectively self-advocate for their learning needs, students need to do several things:

- know how they learn best
- understand why they have certain learning preferences
- communicate learning needs to teachers and peers
- make good decisions in learning activities
- seek assistance from peers and teachers when needed
- model appropriate self-advocacy behaviors for others

You can facilitate and support students' self-advocacy in the following ways:

- encourage open and affirming communication
- model self-advocacy for students—demonstrate confidence and problem-solving skills
- offer resources and information on student rights, support services, and effective communication techniques
- role-play situations for students to practice self-advocacy
- collaborate with support staff, such as counselors, special education teachers, or social workers, to gain advice and resources
- develop a peer mentoring program that connects students to either older students or adults in the community who can assist students in becoming their own best advocate

ESCAPE ROOM ADVENTURE

In this activity, students will work in groups of four to design an escape room by working through a sequence of actions. Students should be grouped so that each group has at least one expert in each of the four learning types from page 21.

Process:

1. As a team, students design their Escape Room Adventure, including the theme, storyline, and characters. (This is where slinkies will shine.)
2. Students work together to write the instructions, rules, and protocols for their Escape Room Adventure. (Paperclips will shine here.)
3. Students set up their Escape Room Adventure, including any puzzles, codes, and pathways to escape. They also predict where participants may need help and come up with ideas for hints when people get stuck. (Here is where magnifying glasses will shine.)
4. After participants have gone through students' adventures, teams reflect on how everything went. (Here is where teddy bears will shine!) Below are some questions for students to reflect upon:
   - How did it feel to work in a team?
   - Were there issues in your collaboration?
   - How did you solve those issues?
   - What plans can you make for next time?

Get Organized

One of the most critical habits of successful people is organization. Organization is the ability to manage materials, information, and time to efficiently and effectively complete tasks. It's a critical self-regulation skill, both in and out of school. But for many students, getting and staying organized is difficult.

When a student lacks organizational skills, their performance suffers and their sense of self-efficacy decreases. Being organized can greatly reduce students' stress and anxiety (affect). It's a learned set of skills (behavior) that helps them control their environments, materials, and daily routines. All this leads to greater confidence for learning, better decision-making, and clearer thinking (cognition).

In this section are ideas for helping students prioritize tasks and get and stay organized. While the organization strategies here are focused on building confidence and getting students ready to learn, you will find additional strategies to help your students stay organized throughout the entire learning cycle on pages 94 and 127.

Strategies for Teachers

Following are ideas for supporting students in getting organized. Students are always watching what you are doing, so setting a good example of organization can be a powerful tool for teaching this skill.

KEEP YOURSELF ORGANIZED

There are a few aspects of this:

- **Ensure that your work area and classroom are clean and organized.** It's unfair to ask students to keep their spaces clean and tidy if yours is a disaster.
- **Keep your classroom well stocked** with pens, pencils, erasers, markers, paper, extra textbooks, additional calculators, and any of the other items students may forget to bring to class. That way, when students forget materials, they won't miss out on learning.
- **Be on time and manage your time well.** See the sections on being on time (page 16) and time management (page 51) for specific ideas.

PROVIDE TIME FOR STUDENTS TO GET ORGANIZED

To help students settle in and prepare themselves for class, devote five minutes at the beginning of each period for students to organize their materials, notes, and mindset. This may also be a helpful strategy when dealing with latecomers. Providing this time for organization helps minimize distractions up front, can improve student focus, and sets a tone for a calm and orderly classroom environment.

You can also use this organizational time in several other ways:

- to check-in with individual students
- to offer a quick re-teach to small groups or individuals
- to provide notes to a student who had been absent
- to collect notes, assignments, or field trip forms
- to take attendance

DEVELOP ORGANIZATIONAL ROUTINES

Predictability in the environment develops a sense of safety and security in the classroom. Established routines promote a positive learning environment by making clear the expectations of the learning community and infusing a sense of order into the learning space.

Try the following routines to encourage organization:

- Provide time throughout the class period for students to check their organization.
- Have students share their notes with partners to ensure they are organized.
- Provide time for students to write in their planners, put notes in folders, or use whatever organizational systems they prefer prior to the end of the class period.
- Post a calendar with important dates—such as when assignments are due, midway check-in points for projects, and when there will be schedule changes.

CHECK IN

Some students need extra support as they practice and develop their organizational skills. You can set aside dedicated time to support students' organization efforts and for students to support and check in with one another.

INTEGRATE ORGANIZATION INTO CONTENT AREAS

Integrating the organizational skills students are learning into your content provides them with extra opportunities to get and stay organized. You can integrate these skills in any curricular area. For example:

- Before writing an essay, discuss a few ways (no more than three) that students might organize their thoughts.
- Prior to beginning group work, assign each student in the group a specific task to perform. Then have students discuss how each group member will contribute to the positive outcome of the group.
- Using a piece of literature, show how a character did or did not organize themselves and what the outcomes were.
- When studying history, have students organize major events into categories.
- Before beginning a lab in science, discuss the various tools needed to complete the task.

Techniques and Tools for Students

To help students improve their attitudes and get themselves ready to learn, share these strategies for organizing their space, materials, resources, and time.

ORGANIZE THE LEARNING SPACE

Clutter of the learning space can clutter the mind. So whether students are working at desks or at tables, in school, at the library, or at home, they should survey the space for clutter before beginning study or an assignment. The checklist on page 127 can help them clear their space and make sure it is clean, distractions are minimized, lighting is good, and unnecessary noises are kept to a minimum. Encourage them to use this checklist, or a similar one, daily.

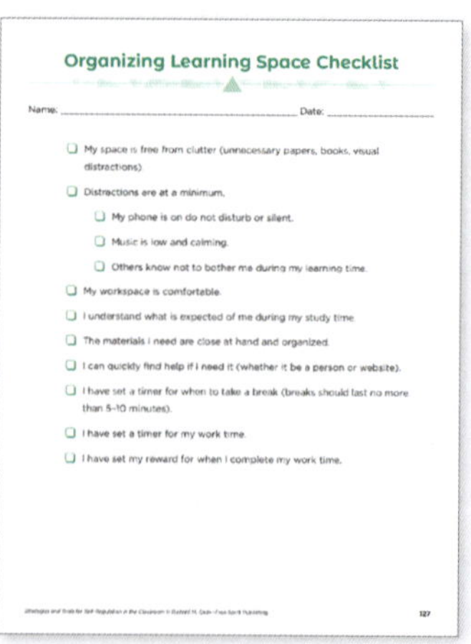

Organizing Learning Space Checklist

Name: ____________________ Date: __________

- ❑ My space is free from clutter (unnecessary papers, books, visual distractions).
- ❑ Distractions are at a minimum.
  - ❑ My phone is on do not disturb or silent.
  - ❑ Music is low and calming.
  - ❑ Others know not to bother me during my learning time.
- ❑ My workspace is comfortable.
- ❑ I understand what is expected of me during my study time.
- ❑ The materials I need are close at hand and organized.
- ❑ I can quickly find help if I need it (whether it be a person or website).
- ❑ I have set a timer for when to take a break (breaks should last no more than 5–10 minutes).
- ❑ I have set a timer for my work time.
- ❑ I have set my reward for when I complete my work time.

127

DEVELOP A ROUTINE

One of the primary benefits of having a routine is the consistency it can bring to a student's life. Regular patterns of behavior help regulate biological rhythms, which in turn make it easier for students to wake up and go to sleep at the same time every day. When students follow a consistent routine, their bodies become accustomed to it, reducing stress and anxiety and getting them ready to learn.

Invite students to spend a day noting the following information:

- when they get up in the morning
- how long it takes them to get dressed and ready for school
- when/what they eat for breakfast
- how long it takes to get to school
- what classes they have
- what time they leave for home
- how they spend their time outside of school
- when (and how much) time they spend studying and getting ready for the next day
- when they go to bed

After seeing a full picture of their day, students can review how they use their time. Encourage them to look for ways to be more efficient with their routines and where they might reduce or increase the time they devote to different aspects of their day. They can share their thoughts with partners or with you if they need assistance.

CREATE A SYSTEM OF ORGANIZATION

An organizational system for schoolwork can help students ensure that everything they need is in one convenient place and that they are clearly recording and prioritizing assignments and tasks. You can help students develop an organizational system that works for them, checking in periodically until they can use it independently. You might share these tools and ideas:

- **Planner.** Many schools offer planners for all students. Help students learn to use them by modeling how to fill out the planner on a daily basis.
- **Calendars.** See the section on being on time (page 16) for ideas.
- **Folders.** Suggest that students use different color folders (virtual or physical) for each subject (red for math; yellow for language arts). They might also choose folder colors based on priority of when work needs to be completed (red for work due the next day; yellow for work due at the end of the week; green for longer term assignments and projects).
- **Multipocket notebook or folder.** Use the various pockets or folders within to organize. For example, work that is due sooner is in pockets nearer the front, while work that has a later due date is nearer the back.
- **Colored pens/highlighters.** In their student planners or on their calendars, students can use different colored pens or highlighters to jot down or highlight what needs to be done in order of priority or by subject.
- **Sticky notes or tabs.** Highlight when projects are due or use flags to highlight what has the highest priority.

USE ASSIGNMENT CHECKLISTS

An assignment checklist can provide a structure and organized way to complete work or a project. It can help students make sure steps are not missed, timelines are met, and work is turned in on time. Knowing what they need to do by when also builds students' confidence in their abilities to control their learning.

Student assignment checklists should include the following categories. A reproducible checklist can be found on page 129.

- **Assignment Description.** In their own words, students should describe the assignment, including the subject area and the teacher's name.
- **Date Due.** Students list the date and time the assignment is due.
- **Midway Check-In Date.** Whether there will be a formal midway check-in with the teacher or not, students can find the point that is midway through the assignment, so they can check in with the teacher, a study buddy, a parent, or themselves to make sure they can complete the assignment on time.
- **Expectations.** Students can put the requirements of the assignment here, the standards or objectives of the assignment, or the categories from the rubric.
- **Obstacles.** Students can list any obstacles they may encounter as they work on the assignment. This can include sporting events, performances, family engagements, limited study time, dealing with siblings, or any other foreseen or predictable hurdles that could come their way.
- **Remedies.** This part of the checklist includes students' plans for how they will overcome or address any of the obstacles they identified. They should list what they may be able to do to ensure they get the assignment completed on time.

PRIORITIZE TASKS

It can be hard for students to stay organized when life gets busy or workloads grow. When students feel overwhelmed by the amount of things they have to do, they may not know where to start or how to move forward, or they may lose sight of what's most important or urgent. You can teach students to use a tool like the Eisenhower Matrix for Managing and Prioritizing Tasks to help them stay on top of what needs attention right away and what they can work on at a later date.

The Eisenhower Matrix for Managing and Prioritizing Tasks

The exact origin of the matrix is unknown, but it is attributed to the leadership lessons from the life of President Dwight D. Eisenhower. Students use the matrix to separate tasks into four categories:

1. Tasks that are urgent and important
2. Tasks that are urgent but not important
3. Tasks that are important but not urgent
4. Tasks that are not important and not urgent

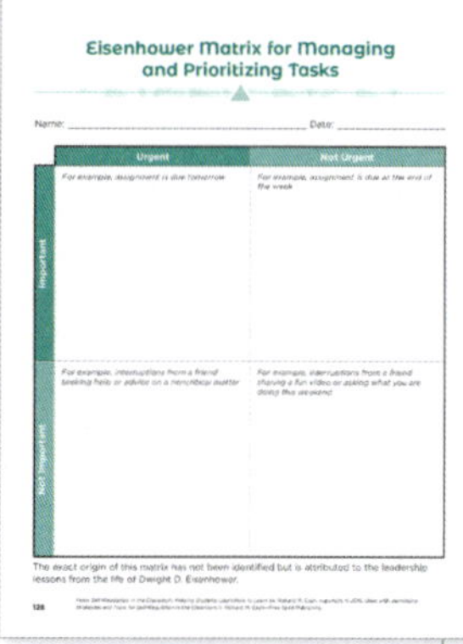

How students classify their tasks will help them determine the order in which to work on them. A reproducible form students can use is available on page 128.

CHUNK LEARNING

Teach students to break work or projects into chunks. Have them review an evening's worth of homework and decide how the work can be broken into chunks based on subjects and priorities (see the Priority Ladder activity below).

PRIORITY LADDER

One way to teach organizational skills is through having students organize or prioritize their thinking, materials, or projects. The Priority Ladder is a useful tool for helping students think through what needs immediate attention and what can wait.

Process:

1. In small groups, using a Priority Ladder handout (see page 130), have students prioritize the items listed below to accomplish any of the following tasks: solve a math problem, find your way home, help you do your home study, survive on a deserted island, teach someone how to cook.
   - battery
   - paperclips
   - pens/pencils
   - notepaper
   - rubber bands
   - ruler
   - permanent markers
   - string
   - pushpins
   - scissors
2. Each team will share how they organized their list and why they put items in the list the way they did. Students will see many creative ways others organized their thinking and materials.
3. Now try this with a list of "what needs to be done," such as a common student workload. In their groups, students list out a typical evening's workload and then place it on a Priority Ladder. They should include the amount of time they will devote to each task, making sure to include breaks. Their list might include the following:
   - five math problems as practice
   - practice speech for language arts
   - read the next chapter in a class novel
   - have parents sign a field trip notice
   - study break
4. Ask students:
   - How do you think prioritizing your workload can help you become a better learner?
   - Why is it important to take breaks during study time?
   - In what ways do you think you can use this strategy in other areas of your life?

Health and Well-Being

Healthy students are happy students. They are more active and possess more positive self-beliefs. So it's no surprise that one of the most effective ways to boost students' confidence and ensure success in learning is by teaching them ways to care for their bodies and minds. Adolescence, the period of life between childhood and adulthood (typically between ages ten and nineteen), is an extremely important time in development. This is the time students set the foundation for the rest of their lives, making it the perfect time for students to begin to build and maintain healthy habits.

Healthy students tend to be more confident because there is a direct correlation between good physical health and positive mental well-being (affect). Healthy students have more positive self-esteem and realistic body image. Students with poor health habits report greater levels of depression and anxiety, especially among adolescent girls (Moksnes and Reidunsdatter 2019). Healthy students are also less likely to engage in risky behaviors, such as smoking and substance use, and are more likely to resist pressure by others to do these things (behavior). Physical health also leads to enhanced cognitive functioning. Exercise stimulates the production of neurotransmitters such as dopamine and serotonin, which are essential for mood regulation and cognitive sharpness. Being healthy also increases blood flow to the brain, promoting learning and memory (cognition).

Those entering adolescence bring with them many vulnerabilities, such as natural risk-seeking, as well as positive resources, like the desire to learn. It is incumbent upon educators to acknowledge both the benefits and susceptibilities of adolescence. While adolescent health is a wide and varied subject, this section will focus on nutrition, physical activity, and mental well-being.

Strategies for Teachers

The role of teachers extends far beyond the walls of the classroom and the subjects they teach. They play a crucial part in shaping the overall development of their students, which includes promoting physical, mental, and emotional health. Helping students maintain their health is essential for their well-being, academic success, and future prospects. The significance of this role cannot be overstated, as the health of the next generation is integral to the prosperity and advancement of society as a whole.

TALK ABOUT NUTRITION

Knowing your community and your students is important here. Don't make assumptions about what students have access to or eat when not at school. Following are a few ideas for modeling nutritional health and supporting students' nutrition in the classroom:

- **Check out the United States Department of Agriculture (nutrition.gov) website** for an amazing set of resources for students and teachers. Take some time to explore the site and even set up an account to receive updated materials and information.
- **Post the MyPlate graphic** (from the USDA site) in your classroom for student reference.
- **Show students what you eat for breakfast, lunch, dinner, and snacks.** Modeling appropriate nutritional choices is critical to students' awareness of the impact food has on their overall health and well-being.

Figure 6: MyPlate Graphic

GET ACTIVE

Another way to support students' health in the classroom is to incorporate more movement into your daily routine and instruction. In addition to movement's effects on physical and mental health, getting their blood pumping can help students stay awake, alert, and engaged in learning. This, in turn, can improve their academic performance. Healthy physical movement can reduce future health issues, lower anxiety and stress, and strengthen bones, muscles, and joints.

Following are a few ideas for how to get students up and moving around:

- **Try improvisation and creative dramatics activities.** These are wonderful and fun ways to get kids up and moving. See pages 12–15 for a few ideas.
- **Adhere to the 10:2/20:2 rule** (see page 10). Use the breaks to get students moving by doing a few jumping jacks or stretches as a group or inviting students to get up and move around the space.
- **Toss a foam ball or crumpled ball of paper back and forth** during class discussion or question-and-answer periods. You may also invite students to stand during these times, even if they aren't answering or asking questions, since simply standing increases blood flow to the brain.
- **Provide fidgets.** Physical activity in the classroom doesn't always have to be grand body movements. Even minor physical movements using hands and fingers can keep the blood moving. Fidgets help reduce stress, assist in avoiding distractions, and increase blood flow.

Well-Being PSAs

Students can create PSAs about chosen well-being topics. For example, maybe they create a video on how to eat healthy, including resources and menu ideas for a healthy diet. Or perhaps they design a poster or a broadcast PSA to share the Four A's of Dealing with Stress (page 41) with peers.

SUPPORT MENTAL WELL-BEING

One of the best ways to boost students' mental health in the classroom is to create a supportive and welcoming learning environment for ALL. (See pages 7–15.) Having an inclusive, caring, and secure learning space ensures that students feel as if they're a part of a community of learners, know they can be themselves, and feel free to make mistakes and take intellectual risks.

Following are a few more ideas for how to support students' mental well-being:

- **Infuse positive well-being into your curriculum and lessons.** This can range from problem-solving techniques to reduce frustration, to communication and collaboration ideas to clarify thinking (see pages 63–68 on listening), to team-building strategies for working well in a group, to discussing how characters in a novel or scientists or other professionals overcame hurdles. Let students know it's okay to be different and to struggle with relationships and ideas. Hard work (effort) is what makes one successful.
- **Provide students with mental health information,** whether through making brochures available in the classroom or hanging posters with phone numbers and website information. This can include information from public health services to community and faith-based groups. No need to make a big deal about them, since many students may be embarrassed to talk about their struggles or want to keep things to themselves.

- **Offer information to students' families and caregivers** about mental well-being resources. This group of supporters may not know how to best promote positive well-being or may question their relevance in the lives of their children. However, significant research states that when adolescents have parental oversight, connectedness, communication, and/or support, they are less likely to engage in risky behaviors (Butler et al. 2022).

Bilateral Stimulation (BLS)

BLS is the process of alternately stimulating the left and right sides of the brain. These neuro-reset activities can help reduce stress, increase physical movement, decrease anxiety, and increase overall feelings of well-being. There are several methods that can be used efficiently in the classroom. Try them with students!

Eye movement. Have students, without moving their heads, look far to the left and then far to the right. They can think about this like watching a game of tennis or ping-pong, without moving their heads. Go back and forth about three times in a row during the class period.

Cross-body tapping. In an upright position, students use their right hands to tap the left sides of their bodies (head, body, legs, feet). Then they switch hands and do the same on the other side. Have students tap about five times on each side. You can also invite them to "pat your stomach while rubbing your head." These ideas are perfect for two-minute brain breaks.

Drumming. On their desks with their left hands, students make a steady beat. With their right hands, they beat a rapid and unsteady beat. Not only does the beating hands increase bilateral stimulation, the sound it creates can also help wake up the brain.

Techniques and Tools for Students

Being healthy, both physically and mentally, has an enormous impact on almost everything students do. A heathy child feels better about themself, lives a more active life, and is more willing to take on academic challenges. Share these ideas with students for how to improve their confidence in learning by focusing on their health.

NUTRITION

The food students eat not only can improve their overall health, but it also has an enormous impact on their academic performance. What students eat (behavior) has an effect on how they feel (affect) and their thinking (cognition). Following are a few ideas for helping students focus on nutrition.

Try a Healthy Week Food Challenge

For one week, have students list everything they consume, from beverages to meals to treats. Then have them organize the foods consumed into the MyPlate model (page 36) to check their balances. Join students by taking the challenge too. (Be sensitive to students who may have a history of eating disorders and offer alternatives or modifications to ensure that the activity feels safe and inclusive, such as having students create a sample food log for a fictional character.)

Share these tips with students for making healthier food choices (USDA, n.d.):

- **Try baked, broiled, grilled, poached, steamed, boiled, or roasted options over fried.** If students are eating out and the preparations are not listed on the menu, they can ask.
- **Add more veggies.** Whether it is mini carrots, celery sticks, or broccoli, eating a crunchy vegetable will help satisfy students' appetites.

- **Add more fruits.** Students can find a couple options that they enjoy, that are easy to carry around in a backpack or bag, and that can be consumed quickly during class breaks. "An apple a day keeps the doctor away" is truth.
- **Scrutinize sauces.** Heavy sauces made with cream or butter, while enjoyable, can be high in unhealthy fats and calories. Ranch dressing is delicious . . . but in moderation!

Survey Cafeteria Staff

Part of focusing on nutrition is knowing where food comes from and how it is managed and prepared. Students might ask questions like these:

- How do you decide on the foods that are offered?
- What regulations do you need to follow?
- Who decides those regulations?
- Where do you get information about healthy diets for students?
- What happens to uneaten foods?
- What foods are least liked by students and why?
- What foods are most liked by students and why?
- How do you ensure that students are eating well?
- What advice would you give to students about eating well?

Students can present their findings to their classmates or another group of students. They may even want to create a poster or advertisement to put up in the cafeteria that promotes healthy eating.

PHYSICAL ACTIVITY

Like nutrition, a student's physical activity is directly related to their physical and mental health. What students do physically (behavior) impacts how they feel (affect) and their thinking (cognition), so being physically active can be a tool to improve mental health. The brain needs physical movement to acquire and process information. In this way, physical activity can also improve academic performance (CDC 2025). Following are a few ideas to help students get active.

Track Activity

There are many apps available to help people do this. Have each student download one they like and keep track of their activity each day. They may even want to journal how they feel when they are active versus inactive. Ask, "Do you find a relationship between your behavior and your feelings?" General guidelines recommend that students do at least 60 minutes of physical activity each day (CDC 2024).

Try a Healthy Week Physical Challenge

Just like the Healthy Week Food Challenge, for one week, have your students list everything they do physically throughout the day. This can be anything—from quick morning exercise to going from class to class to sports practice or swimming lessons. Students can use an app to chart their steps and other physical actions or keep track in a notebook. After students have one week of data, consider making a competition the next week to see who (or which team of students) can increase their physical activity the most, rather than who can be the most active. This ensures the competition is fair and inclusive for students who may have limited physical mobility or who do not participate in after-school sports. Encourage students to note how they feel when they are active versus inactive. You can join your students in this challenge as well!

Incorporate Movement Activities

There are many kinds of physical activities students can try. Teach students that it's generally best to start with a lower level of intensity and build themselves up to higher levels of intensity the stronger they get. Provide these examples of activities at the three intensity levels:

moderate-intensity activities

- practicing gentle forms of yoga or chair yoga
- brisk walking
- bicycle riding
- hiking
- swimming
- playing baseball, softball, or basketball
- performing water aerobics
- hand cycling

high-intensity activities

- running
- bicycle riding that includes hills
- skateboarding
- jumping rope
- cross-country running or skiing
- playing football or soccer
- playing tennis
- performing rapid arm movements
- boxing
- stationary arm biking
- dancing

strength-training activities

- weightlifting
- using resistance bands
- practicing vigorous forms of yoga
- doing calisthenics: sit-ups, push-ups, jumping jacks
- doing medicine ball workouts
- doing bodyweight exercises (such as push-ups, planks, and leg lifts tailored to a student's mobility)

MENTAL WELL-BEING

Students' mental well-being, or how they think about themselves (cognition), affects what they do (behavior) and how they feel (affect). Adolescence is a wonderful time of life full of exploration, new friendships, and creativity. It's also a time when students' lives may be full of conflict, strange feelings, and distractions. Stress can be a particularly challenging part of this time as well.

Following are strategies students can use to care for their mental well-being.

Recognize and Combat Stress

Stress is the body's natural response to intense physical, emotional, or mental demands. Signs students are stressed can include headaches, body pains that don't seem normal, digestive problems, sleep issues, sustained sadness or depression, weight loss or gain, autoimmune issues, or skin changes. Share page 131 with students to help them recognize their signs of stress.

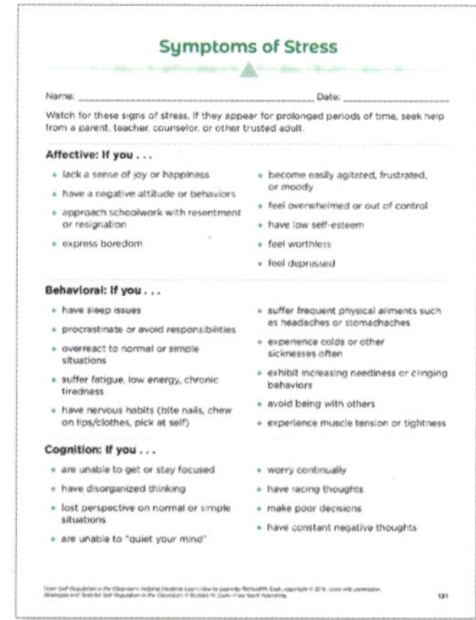

Symptoms of Stress

Name: ______________________ Date: __________

Watch for these signs of stress. If they appear for prolonged periods of time, seek help from a parent, teacher, counselor, or other trusted adult.

Affective: If you . . .

- lack a sense of joy or happiness
- have a negative attitude or behaviors
- approach schoolwork with resentment or resignation
- express boredom
- become easily agitated, frustrated, or moody
- feel overwhelmed or out of control
- have low self-esteem
- feel worthless
- feel depressed

Behavioral: If you . . .

- have sleep issues
- procrastinate or avoid responsibilities
- overreact to normal or simple situations
- suffer fatigue, low energy, chronic tiredness
- have nervous habits (bite nails, chew on lips/clothes, pick at self)
- suffer frequent physical ailments such as headaches or stomachaches
- experience colds or other sicknesses often
- exhibit increasing neediness or clinging behaviors
- avoid being with others
- experience muscle tension or tightness

Cognition: If you . . .

- are unable to get or stay focused
- have disorganized thinking
- lost perspective on normal or simple situations
- are unable to "quiet your mind"
- worry continually
- have racing thoughts
- make poor decisions
- have constant negative thoughts

131

Once students learn to recognize the signs they're stressed, they can identify some strategies they might use to effectively cope when life gets stressful. You can share the following Four A's of Dealing with Stress. Which of the tips might students use to limit or cope with stress in their lives?

Get Enough Sleep

One of the most important factors in maintaining mental (as well as physical) well-being is getting enough sleep. Research suggests that a quality night's sleep of between nine and twelve hours for school-age kids and eight to ten hours for teens is preferable (KidsHealth 2021). Students can keep a running journal of their sleep for a week, noting whether they had a good or bad night's sleep each night and how they felt the next day.

To support a good night's rest, students can try to set and follow a consistent sleep schedule—winding down and going to bed around the same time most nights. You can also share these strategies:

- **Create a bedtime ritual.** Students can do something each night that helps their brain unwind from the day, such as reading a book or listening to calming music.
- **Avoid screens for at least thirty minutes before going to bed.** Beyond the possible effects of screen light the body's natural cycle, scrolling through social media can overstimulate the brain, increase anxiety, and make it harder to wind down for restful sleep.
- **Avoid caffeine and sugar for at least two hours before bed.** Caffeine and sugar, when digesting, can increase heart rate and blood pressure, making it difficult to relax and fall asleep.
- **Adjust sleeping arrangements.** The best sleeping environments are cool, dark, and quiet. This may not always be the case in students' homes. Using a pair of earplugs or noise-canceling headphones and a sleep mask can be ways to correct the environment for good sleep.
- **Limit nap times.** Naps should be between ten and thirty minutes. Longer naps can cause grogginess and may disrupt nighttime sleep. Students should try not to nap after 4 p.m.
- **Stay active during the day.** This can increase the likelihood of a good night's sleep. If students had a day without a lot of physical activity, they might try a relaxing walk after school or in the early evening.

The Four A's of Dealing with Stress

Avoid unnecessary stress by managing your time:

- Learn to say "no."
- Analyze your schedule to allow for downtime.
- Set plans and know your deadlines.

Alter the situation:

- Advocate for what you need.
- Take your power back (using "I" language to stay in control: "I don't like the way I'm being spoken to").
- Learn to compromise (whether it be with others or with yourself).

Adapt to the stressors:

- Think positively. It can have a great effect on how you deal with stress.
- Use affirmative language ("I feel best when I can use my computer to compose my thoughts" rather than "I don't like writing down my thoughts").
- Look at the big picture, or "Don't sweat the small stuff" (learn to see the forest rather than each tree).

Accept what you can't change:

- Be accountable for your actions, not expecting others to react to your lack of planning.
- Find the silver lining or learn from the situation ("Oh well, I won't do that again.").
- Remember: NO ONE is perfect.

- **Practice yoga or do stretching exercises before bed.** These exercises can release tension and prepare students for a good night's sleep. They are also good activities to do in the morning to get ready for the day ahead.

Deep Breathing

Encourage students to try this exercise several times throughout the day. It is also a good exercise to use as they're falling asleep.

1. With eyes closed, breathe in through the nose—thinking "relax."
2. Hold for three seconds—thinking "relax."
3. Exhale through the mouth—thinking "relax."

BEING HEALTHY BINGO

Being healthy doesn't have to be a chore. Being Healthy Bingo can teach students fun new ways to be healthy and encourage them to try them.

Preparation: You'll need to print enough copies of the Being Healthy Bingo card on page 132 for each student in your group. The Bingo card can be manipulated to add activities you have been working on in class. Mix up the activities in the boxes so that each student or team will have a different version of the card.

Process:

1. Hand out Being Healthy Bingo cards to students.
2. Explain the rules of Bingo if students don't already know them and share guidelines for your game, including how long you will play for (a week or longer to give students enough time to get a bingo) and the different patterns they can try for (blackout, four corners, diagonal, straight across, up/down).
3. Students should let you know as they achieve Bingos during the game. You may want to offer small prizes or incentives for filling out their cards.
4. Once the Bingo time period is over, discuss:
   - What did you learn about yourself and your health habits?
   - What may be an area of health you want to improve on?
   - In what ways can you make your health more fun?
   - Who might you collaborate with (a parent, a friend, a teacher) on getting healthy?

PART II:
Setting and Managing Learning Goals

Some students seem to be born goal setters. They know what they want to do and how to prioritize, and they are internally motivated to find success in what they have set their minds to accomplish. More often, students need support and structures to learn how to set goals, prioritize tasks, and stay focused on what's important—and that's totally normal.

One of the most challenging aspects of developing strong self-regulation for learning is learning to set and manage goals. It is also one of the most crucial. In fact, longitudinal research suggests that high-achieving students tend to be more self-regulated and possess the strategic skills of goal setting, using time wisely, and preparing for challenges (Biemiller and Meichenbaum 2017).

Determining which students have natural or more independent abilities to set and manage goals versus those who need greater support is more of an art than a science. It requires you to listen to students as they discuss their work habits, performances, and product evaluations and measure how they feel about their work. (Did they know what to do and were they able to answer their own questions upon reflection?) Those who are more affectively (emotionally) engaged know how to do what is expected, are self-directed, and are more likely to set and manage reasonable learning goals. Those who have lower affect engagement rely on the teacher to direct their actions and tend to be more dependent learners. And they need more assistance in setting and managing goals.

The strategies in this section support you in teaching all students to set learning goals, manage their time to achieve those goals, and plan for and overcome obstacles in learning.

Learning Goals

Learning is a complex process. It goes well beyond just memorizing a lot of facts and applying them to a test. Learning is best done when students are trying to accomplish something that doesn't have one right way of doing or one right answer. It requires students to hold in mind what is necessary and what is possible. It's an open-ended opportunity for students to use their experiences in the classroom to further their knowledge and intellectual curiosity. As such, a focus on what they want to do or accomplish—on the goal of learning—is essential.

This section is centered on helping students set goals with a focus on learning. A goal is either something a person aspires to accomplish or a desired outcome. The person setting the goal must understand what is realistic to accomplish—those outcomes that are doable. Students who haven't encountered much classroom success usually have difficulty understanding what outcomes are attainable and appropriate, so goal setting can be quite challenging for them.

Learning goals can have a profound impact on student achievement. Numerous studies have shown the benefits of appropriate goal setting. In fact, students who set challenging, yet achievable, goals are significantly more self-directed learners and have higher degrees of achievement motivation (Hematian, Rezaei, and Mohammadyfar 2017). Goal setting can increase students' self-confidence and support a positive attitude (affect), focus their attention on what needs to be done through hard work (behavior), and define the plan or purpose for learning (cognition). Additionally, setting goals helps students stay organized, assists in time management, increases motivation, and makes them feel good when goals are achieved.

Strategies for Teachers

Goal setting should be something students do often and can easily manage. When goal setting fails, it's because the goal was too grandiose, cumbersome, unachievable, or unworthy of the attention needed to accomplish it. Following are strategies for teaching students to set realistic goals that are worth the effort. Chapter 6 in *Self-Regulation in the Classroom: Helping Students Learn How to Learn* shares additional ways to guide students in goal setting, as well as several graphic organizers that can assist in the goal-setting process.

DO A BOOK STUDY

Look for books about individuals who set and achieved (or did not achieve) goals. A simple internet search for "books for adolescents on setting goals" will yield hundreds of options at various reading levels. As you read such a book, focus on identifying the goal, the steps the individual took to achieve it, and what worked and didn't work for them.

Take, for example, the book *Serena Williams: Inspiring Young Athletes* by James C. Oliver. The book, written for ages five to fifteen, takes readers along on the journey of tennis star Serena Williams. After reading the book, have students discuss some of the questions below:

- What challenges did Serena Williams face throughout her life, especially in her early years?
- How did her presence in a sport dominated by people who didn't look like her help change people's perception of tennis?
- How did Serena break barriers through her hard work?
- What role did goal setting play in Serena's successes both on and off the court?
- In what ways do you see yourself in Serena's life story?
- What lessons can you learn from Serena's journey?

START WITH PERSONAL GOALS

When teaching students to set learning goals, have them start by setting a goal for something they want to do for themselves. A goal needs to have value to the student to make achieving it worth their time and effort.

A good place to start is by having them consider personal goals in four categories: academic growth, personal growth, health and fitness growth, and growth toward ideal self. These categories are based on work by psychologist Carl Rogers (1951) and numerous business professionals. Have your students select one of the categories and create a goal. Then help them fine-tune what they would like to accomplish using the SMARTS/S method (page 47).

Following are examples of student goals in each of the four categories:

1. Academic growth (learning something new): "I want to learn to play the flute."
2. Personal growth (being a better communicator): "I want to get along better with my sister."
3. Health and fitness growth (increasing health): "I want to run three times per week to support my physical and mental health."
4. Growth toward ideal self (being a better me): "I want to become a better friend by growing my listening skills."

Techniques and Tools for Students

Successful people routinely set goals based on what they want to accomplish and plan for how they will achieve those goals. Following are some goal-setting tips to share with students.

START SMALL

When teaching students to set learning goals, encourage them to start small by noting one thing they want to do each day. This can be as simple as "Be nice to my teammates" or "Avoid looking at my phone for at least one class period." Direct students to refer to this small goal throughout the day to remind themselves of what they'd like to accomplish. At the end of the day, encourage students to reflect on their goals by asking themselves these questions:

- Did I achieve my goal?
  - If yes, what made me successful in achieving the goal?
  - If no, what got in the way of achieving the goal?
- How does it feel to have met (or not met) my goal?
- What did I do that assisted me in reaching or not reaching my goal?
- What will I plan to do tomorrow?

FOLLOW A GOAL-SETTING METHOD

It is helpful to introduce various methods students can follow to guide the process of setting learning goals. Following a goal-setting method can help keep students focused on what they want to achieve and better define how they can get there.

SMARTS/S Goal Setting

SMARTS/S is an acronym that can be used to aid students in focusing their efforts on what they want to accomplish. The SMARTS/S structure helps students define *what* they will do, *how* they will do it, and *why* it's important. When teaching the SMARTS/S method, start with setting personal goals, then move into academic goal setting.

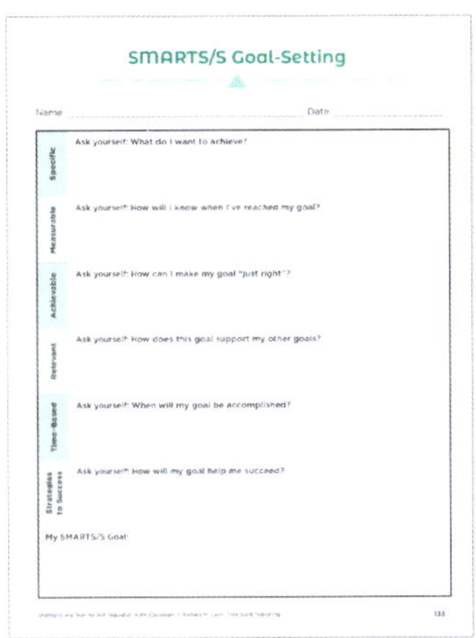

SMARTS/S Goal-Setting

Name Date

Specific	Ask yourself: What do I want to achieve?
Measurable	Ask yourself: How will I know when I've reached my goal?
Achievable	Ask yourself: How can I make my goal "just right"?
Relevant	Ask yourself: How does this goal support my other goals?
Time-Based	Ask yourself: When will my goal be accomplished?
Strategies to Success	Ask yourself: How will my goal help me succeed?

My SMARTS/S Goal:

133

It's best to use the SMARTS/S method in a step-by-step manner. Start with S and move through each of the letters until students feel comfortable with the process. You can differentiate the acronym to meet students' needs. For example, if you are working with younger students or students who need greater support with setting goals, you may choose to do only the letters SMT. For students needing an average level of support, you may want to do SMART. With more advanced goal setters, try the entire acronym. A form students can use when setting SMARTS/S goals is on page 133.

Here's what the acronym stands for:

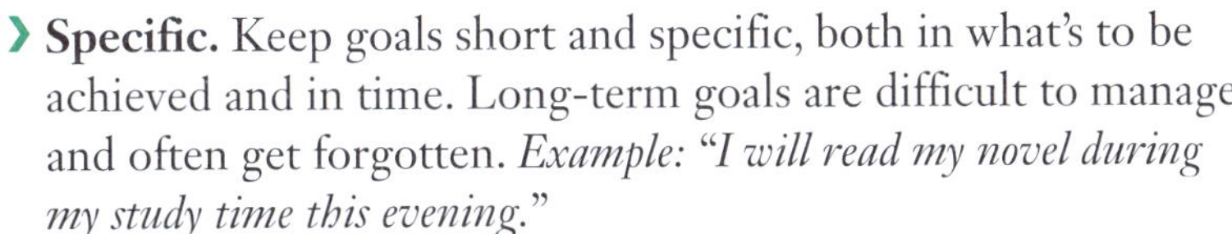

- **Specific.** Keep goals short and specific, both in what's to be achieved and in time. Long-term goals are difficult to manage and often get forgotten. *Example: "I will read my novel during my study time this evening."*
- **Measurable.** It's important for students to know when they have reached their goals. Being able to count what they have done or how much they need to do to get to the goal can be motivating. This is the "how much" and "for how long." *Example: "I will read ten pages of my novel during my study time this evening."*
- **Achievable.** Setting a goal that is too high or too low can be disastrous. Learning goals need to fit the "Goldilocks Principle"; they need to be "just right." This means the goal requires some effort and is worthy of the student's time. *Example: "In the past, I've been able to read eight pages during my study time. Reading ten pages of my novel during my study time will be the 'just-right' challenge for me."*
- **Relevant.** A goal should be aligned to what needs to be accomplished or connected to a long-term objective. It should also be something that the student wants to achieve or that will set them on the path to a better future. *Example: "In the past, I've been able to read eight pages during my study time. Reading ten pages of my novel during my study time will be the 'just-right' challenge for me and will benefit me during discussion time tomorrow."*
- **Time-based.** Similar to the "measurable" part of the goal, this is about setting the time for when goal should be achieved. For students, it's better to keep this date in the near future. Adolescents live in the moment; long-term goals don't often work well for them. *Example: "In the past, I've been able to read eight pages during my study time. Reading ten pages of my novel during my study time, from 7:30 to 8:30 this evening, will be the 'just-right' challenge for me and will benefit me during discussion time tomorrow."*
- **Strategies to Success.** The most sophisticated level of goal setting includes building from strategies (discrete conscious actions) to skills (automaticity). Knowing how a "strategy" builds to a "skill" is essential in the learning process. This is the *why* of learning. In the example, not only has the learner acknowledged how accomplishing the reading before class can improve their ability to discuss the reading during class, but they have also noted that they gained a deeper understanding of the author's intent. *Example: "In the past, I've been able to read eight pages during my study time. Reading ten pages of my novel during my study time, from 7:30 to 8:30 this evening, will be the 'just-right' challenge for me and will benefit me during discussion time and help me gain a better understanding of what the author intended."*

D3R: Four-Question Goal Setting

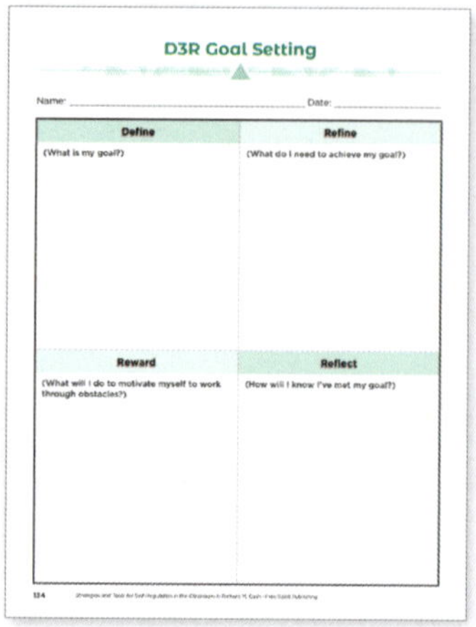
D3R Goal Setting

Name: Date:

Define	Refine
(What is my goal?)	(What do I need to achieve my goal?)
Reward	**Reflect**
(What will I do to motivate myself to work through obstacles?)	(How will I know I've met my goal?)

D3R is a structure students can use when they're learning how to set goals. This method can help them stay focused, reflect on what they have accomplished, and find ways to reward their efforts. It is best used with short-term goals, such as goals for home study each night. A D3R Goal Setting form is on page 134.

Here's how the method works:

1. **Define. What is your goal?** Encourage students to be as specific as possible when they define their goals. Goals shouldn't be too big or unrealistic ("I want to make a million dollars by the time I'm twenty years old"). Nor should they be too small or insignificant ("I will stay awake in Mrs. Johnson's class for the next ten minutes"). Students can use the Goldilocks Principle to define a goal that's just right ("I want to complete the next chapter during my home study period tonight").
2. **Refine. What do you need to achieve your goal?** In this step, students determine what they need to accomplish their goals. For the just-right goal identified above, students will need to have a quiet space, proper lighting, the book, sticky notes, and a pen/pencil.
3. **Reward. What will you do when there are distractions and interruptions, or when you just lose motivation to complete the work?** Students can also think of this as a reward system for persevering through challenges. They can put together a quick list:
    - **Avoid distractions and interruptions.** For example, students can turn their phone off or turn it upside down, let their family and friends know they need thirty minutes of quiet time, gather any snacks or drinks they might need before starting, and so on.
    - **Stay motivated.** Waning motivation is a natural response to things that are challenging. When motivation starts to decline, it's time to take a break. Students could go for a quick walk, do some deep breathing, exercise, grab a snack, or get a drink of water.
    - **Reward themselves.** If students are studying for thirty minutes, every ten minutes they stay focused, they can give themselves a little reward—such as a quick look at their phone, a snack, or a favorite beverage. This mini break should stay under two minutes!
4. **Reflect. How will you know you've met your goal?** At the end of study time, students can do a quick check. Teach them to ask themselves the following:
    - Did I do what I set out to do?
    - What did I learn about the topic and myself?
    - How does it feel to have met (or not met) my goal?
    - What is my plan for next time?

The Four P's of Goal Setting

The Four P's of Goal Setting, created by Leaders Excellence, provide a comprehensive framework for creating and achieving meaningful goals. Incorporating the four P's into the goal-setting process can significantly enhance students' abilities to achieve success. Whether they are setting personal or academic goals, the four P's can guide them toward fulfilling their potential and accomplishing what they set out to do.

Here's what the P's stand for:

1. **Positive.** It's important that students frame their goals positively. Goals should be based on something that students want to accomplish and that makes them a better person. Rather than "I will not get a poor grade on this test," a positive goal would be "I will do my very best to get a good grade on this test."
2. **Personal.** Setting goals can be a way for students to focus on *who* or *how* they want to be rather than on *what* they want to be. They can focus on making their goals about things that will improve not only their academic performance but also their personal qualities. For example: "By putting effort forward to get a good grade on this test, my focus will be on learning to be patient, persistent, and responsible."
3. **Possible.** Students must ensure that their goals are achievable and worth the effort. When goals are too lofty or unrealistic, they may not be achieved, which may lead students to feel disappointed or as if they have failed. It's also easy to quickly lose motivation for goals that are out of reach. For example, if a student sets a goal to be a professional baseball player, but they lack the skills and abilities to be a pro, then they are leading themself down a lonely and disappointing path. In identifying goals, students should evaluate their talents, abilities, and desires. Putting effort forward to be the best they can be is realistic. A better goal would be, "Through practice and commitment, I will try out for and make the baseball team this spring."
4. **Priority.** No person can do *everything* they might possibly want to do in the time they have available to them. Students can list what they need and want to achieve, and then prioritize their lists based on what must be done first, second, third, and so on. Remember, not everything can happen right away, so teach students to create "parking lot" lists—those things they would like to achieve when they have the time and/or opportunity.

GOAL-SETTING PRACTICE

The activities that follow are meant to guide students through a fun process of setting and managing goals. The first activity ("To a Mouse") can show students how not having a goal can make things go wrong. This activity can also support building a positive attitude and be used to help students overcome hurdles in their planning and management of goals. The second activity (D3R Using a Folktale) has students analyze goal setting and management using the D3R method.

"TO A MOUSE": WHAT COULD GO WRONG?

Process:

1. Read this excerpt from the Robert Burns poem "To a Mouse":

   The best-laid schemes of mice and men
   Go oft awry,
   And leave us nothing but grief and pain,
   For promised joy!

2. Discuss with students what they think these lines mean. How may this have happened to them? How might a plan go awry? What can be done to ensure that a plan is carried out for "promised joy"?

3. Present the TSAP chart (page 135) to students with the example filled in. Explain the terms listed (you are welcome to put other terms that are most problematic for your students in the graphic). Explain the difference between a synonym and an antonym.
4. Demonstrate how to use the antonyms to avoid the terms to create a positive plan (goal).
5. If time allows, encourage students to come up with up to five more terms that may impact their ability to set and achieve their goals.
6. Reinforce for students that negative terms can be turned around to create a positive plan of action.

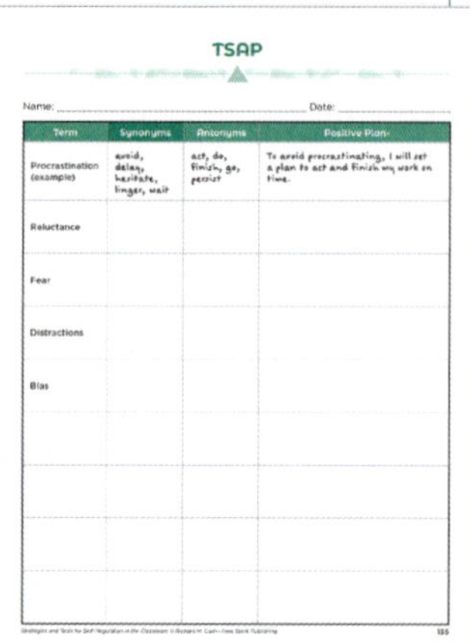
TSAP

Name: Date:

Term	Synonyms	Antonyms	Positive Plan
Procrastination (example)	avoid, delay, hesitate, linger, wait	act, do, finish, go, persist	To avoid procrastinating, I will set a plan to act and finish my work on time.
Reluctance			
Fear			
Distractions			
Bias			

D3R USING A FOLKTALE

Process:

1. Individually or as a group, have students read Aesop's fable "The Tortoise and the Hare." You can easily find this fable online.
2. Have each student select either Tortoise or Hare. They will analyze the character's goal-setting process using the D3R method. If needed, provide this example for Hare:
   - Define: Hare wanted to win the race.
   - Refine: Hare believed all he needed to win the race was speed.
   - Reward: Hare thought that the reward would be to make fun of Tortoise.
   - Reflect: Hare didn't win the race, not reaching his goal.
3. Now invite students to reflect on their chosen character's goal-setting experience. You can use the questions below, or similar:
   - Did your character do what they set out to do?
   - What did your character learn about themself?
   - How do you think your character feels to have met or not met their goal?
   - What should be your character's plan for next time?
4. Have students work together to discuss their findings.
5. To extend this activity, you can have students do any of the following:
   - Rewrite the fable so that Hare does a better job at setting and managing his goal.
   - Discuss other lessons learned from the fable.
   - Suggest what Fox could have done to be a better judge or coach.
   - Write their own fables about setting and managing a goal.

Time Management

During the school day, kids rush from one subject to another, one classroom to another, barely squeezing in enough time for a snack or lunch. In many schools, recess and downtime have been eliminated or greatly reduced to allow for more instructional time. After school, students may be involved in extracurricular activities, such as sports, theater, and music lessons, or may attend child care. Once home, students then must spend time studying or doing outside-of-school work. When kids finally do have downtime, it's time for bed. Their developing brains have not had any chance to power down, relax, reflect on the day, or spend time doing "nothing."

Time has always been a factor in learning, whether it is that students have too little time for learning or too much time between learning activities. Managing one's time for learning effectively plays a crucial role in self-regulation. It fosters emotional stability, motivation, discipline, initiative, focus, and strategic thinking (cognition). When time is managed well (behavior), students feel less stress, are able to accomplish their goals, and have a more positive outlook for the future (affect). Therefore, it is incumbent upon educators to teach students how to set time limits and manage their time wisely to avoid burnout and distraction.

The focus of this section is on how to assist students in managing their time to meet their learning goals, and especially on the time students put forward during the learning process. Strategies for scheduling and being on time can be found in part I (page 16).

Strategies for Teachers

Most students are going to need assistance in managing their time for learning. There are specific techniques and strategies you can employ in the classroom to provide a structure for time management. You'll see there is some overlap of strategies listed in this and other sections. This is to reinforce the strength of the strategy and show how it is necessary for both academic performance and life after school.

ESTABLISH CLASSROOM ROUTINES

Being consistent with class time can be beneficial for students who are developing time-management skills. When they know what, where, and when things are going to happen, they can do a better job of planning their own time. Also, posting reminders of when assignments are due, as well as other events and obligations, is extremely important for keeping students on track.

SET REALISTIC AND CLEAR DEADLINES

Make sure your students know when assignments are due. And be realistic in your expectations for how long it will take students to complete your assignments. Deadlines that are unrealistic (having a due date that is too soon or too far out) don't support students in planning and can stress them out. Unrealistic deadlines also stifle creativity and decrease enjoyment. When setting due dates for assignments or projects, try to be mindful of what exactly you're asking students to do and of the many outside responsibilities they have, from after-school activities and sports to family commitments and part-time jobs.

Being clear and specific about deadlines helps students prioritize what needs to be done and when, leaving them feeling confident that they can get their work in on time and achieve their learning goals. It can also be a way to motivate students who tend to procrastinate. You can even provide them with a countdown or calendar to help them plan.

Here are some things to keep in mind:

- **Make sure the dates and times are clear,** so everyone knows when things are due.
- **Be specific about what is due** and how it needs to be submitted (online, hard copy).
- **Consider multiple ways of communicating deadlines** to students and families, such as in writing, on a calendar, in multiple languages, and via text, email, phone calls, or newsletters.
- **Be consistent with how you set deadlines** and how assignments need to be submitted.
- **Use a calendar system** that encourages students to track upcoming due dates and manage their work effectively (see Being on Time in part I, page 16).
- **Establish ways for students to advocate for themselves** when they need additional time, resources, or support.
- **Be fair with consequences when deadlines aren't met.** Fair consequences consider what the student may be dealing with in their outside-of-school life, as well as their academic needs.

CHUNK ASSIGNMENTS

Breaking down larger assignments and projects into smaller chunks can help students manage their time and achieve learning goals without overwhelming them. Note in your timeline the dates for when each chunk needs to be completed. Offer assistance when students fall behind or miss an objective and provide resources to help them complete the chunk. It may also be helpful for students to set and follow a Priority Ladder (see page 130) to get a project completed on time. Doing so can help students stay focused on the product (the goal) as well as the process (the management of the goal).

Techniques and Tools for Students

Setting and managing learning goals can be a daunting process for students. Share the ideas below with students to help them manage their time for learning.

FOCUS ON ONE THING AT A TIME

Technically, the human brain can only pay attention to one thing at a time. While it's true that students may be able to do several things at once, their brains can only focus higher-order processing on one thing at a time. When students try to do too many things simultaneously, they're actually lessening their productivity, making more mistakes, and losing time switching from one thing to another. Students can use Priority Ladders (page 130) to set steps for achieving the goals they've set for themselves and ensure that they're focusing on one thing at a time.

IDENTIFY OPTIMAL LEARNING TIME

Whether seconds are dragging or hours are flying by, all time is the same. A minute studying a complex math equation may seem long, while a minute riding a roller coaster may seem fast, but both are equal in duration. Neuroscience is teaching us a lot about human perceptions of time and how to best utilize learning time. The science of chronobiology explores how all human organisms are affected by the day-night cycle of the earth's rotations. Understanding their natural circadian rhythms, which last about twenty-four hours, can assist students in knowing when it's best to exert themselves physically and intellectually. For more on teaching this concept to students, see the activity at the end of this chapter. Also share the Study Q&A on page 137.

Study Q&A

Q: When is the best time to study?

A: The optimal time to study depends on your natural patterns of activity and sleep.

- **Morning study time** may be beneficial if you have had a good night's sleep. The brain tends to be sharpest in the morning, especially after a good breakfast. In addition, the natural sunlight is good for your eyes and for gaining vitamin D. You can use morning study time to learn something new or review notes from the day before.
- **Afternoon study time** is a time for the brain to integrate new information with what you already know. Since this is the time after school, you can use it to reflect on what you have learned throughout the day and what you remember. It's also a good time to connect with peers in a study group or to contact someone who can help you when you get stuck. Plus, libraries will be open if you need more information.
- **Night study time** is generally not the most effective time to learn. Based on how you feel at the end of the day, you may be more likely to concentrate on difficult content at night or it may be best to leave it for the next day.

Q: How long should I study?

A: You are the best judge of your own concentration and how much energy you have available. But, in general, follow the ten-minute rule. Try to study for ten minutes per your grade level each night. For example:

- Third grade: 30 minutes
- Fourth grade: 40 minutes
- Fifth grade: 50 minutes
- Middle school (grades 6–8): 60 minutes
- High school (grades 9–12): 90 to 120 minutes

Q: What if I need to work longer than the ten-minute rule?

A: Some research suggests that doing more may actually be doing less. A study by the Stanford Graduate School of Education found that students in some of the highest performing high schools who spent more than 120 minutes studying did not gain greater academic success. In fact, some students who did more than three hours of homework "experienced . . . more academic stress, physical health problems, and lack of balance in their lives" (Galloway, Conner, and Pope 2013, 490).

continued

137

TAKE BREAKS

Taking breaks during learning can be a powerful technique to avoid distraction and burnout. Breaks allow the brain to process information (see the 10:1/10:2 rule on page 10). Additionally, taking breaks improves physical and mental health, increases motivation, boosts creativity, improves memory, offers time for reflection and clarity, prevents fatigue, improves concentration, and increases productivity.

Breaks can pose a problem, however, if students don't know how to get back on track. Teach students productive ways to set time limits for their breaks (between two and five minutes), such as setting a timer or timing how long it takes to walk around the block. Also, help them set limits on the amount of time they dedicate to studying between breaks.

TRY A RESET

Sometimes students need a reset or restart when working to achieve a goal or on a big project. Try these steps to help students reboot when frustration sets in.

1. Ask questions about the student's affect, behavior, and cognition to find out where the learning block may be happening:
   - Affect: What are you feeling right now about the project/goal? Are your feelings getting in the way?
   - Behavior: What are you doing that isn't working? Can you think of another way to approach the project/goal?
   - Cognition: What thoughts do you have about the project/goal? Do you need to do some more thinking and planning to ensure you are going in the right direction?
2. Review the student's goal and their plan for achieving it, or the project objectives and learning outcomes. Keep the focus on what the student wants to achieve or on the purpose of the project.
3. Reinforce their self-efficacy. Some students may get stuck when they think they don't have the tools needed to achieve their goals or complete a project.
4. Offer background information or resources to jumpstart their work. It may be that the student is frustrated because they don't have all the materials or resources they need.

After a reset, students will likely feel refreshed, recharged, and able to commit to staying focused.

KNOW YOUR CHRONOTYPE

The science of chronobiology informs us that all human organisms are affected by the day-night cycle of the earth's rotations. A person's chronotype is their natural tendency to feel tired or alert at certain times. It is determined by someone's personal internal clock, which guides their circadian rhythm (Medichron Publications, n.d.). Understanding their own chronotype and circadian rhythm, which lasts about twenty-four hours, can assist students in knowing when it's best to exert themselves physically and intellectually.

Process:

1. Have students take the Chronotype Survey on page 139.
2. After they finish the survey, share the Chronotype Tips on page 141.

3. Have students gather in like and unlike groups. They read the tips together and discuss strategies for how they can manage themselves.
4. In their like and unlike groups, students discuss ways they can work with, not against, the needs and expectations of the learning process.

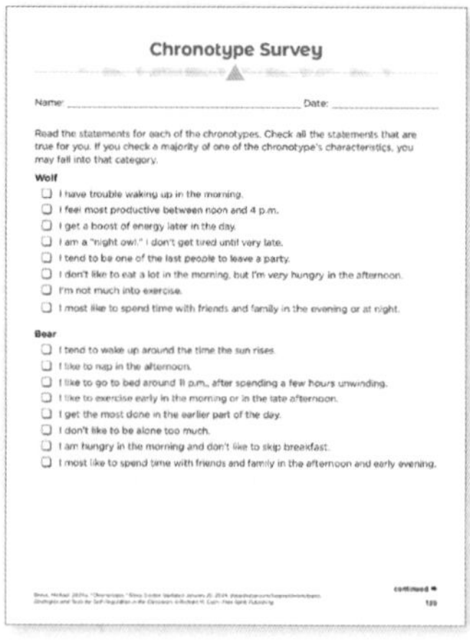

Chronotype Survey

Name: ____________________ Date: ____________

Read the statements for each of the chronotypes. Check all the statements that are true for you. If you check a majority of one of the chronotype's characteristics, you may fall into that category.

Wolf

- ❑ I have trouble waking up in the morning.
- ❑ I feel most productive between noon and 4 p.m.
- ❑ I get a boost of energy later in the day.
- ❑ I am a "night owl." I don't get tired until very late.
- ❑ I tend to be one of the last people to leave a party.
- ❑ I don't like to eat a lot in the morning, but I'm very hungry in the afternoon.
- ❑ I'm not much into exercise.
- ❑ I most like to spend time with friends and family in the evening or at night.

Bear

- ❑ I tend to wake up around the time the sun rises.
- ❑ I like to nap in the afternoon.
- ❑ I like to go to bed around 11 p.m., after spending a few hours unwinding.
- ❑ I like to exercise early in the morning or in the late afternoon.
- ❑ I get the most done in the earlier part of the day.
- ❑ I don't like to be alone too much.
- ❑ I am hungry in the morning and don't like to skip breakfast.
- ❑ I most like to spend time with friends and family in the afternoon and early evening.

continued ➡

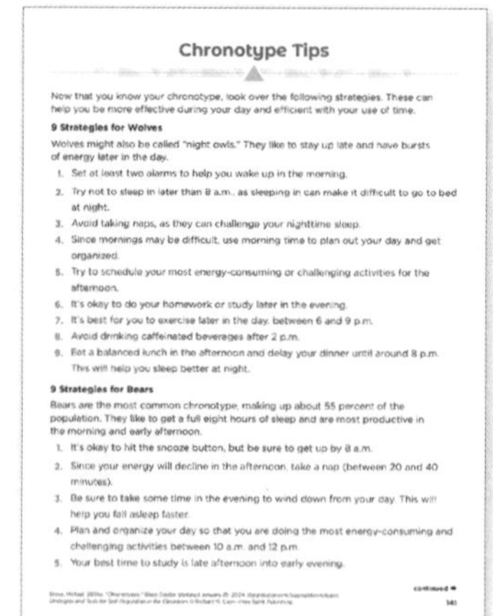

Chronotype Tips

Now that you know your chronotype, look over the following strategies. These can help you be more effective during your day and efficient with your use of time.

9 Strategies for Wolves

Wolves might also be called "night owls." They like to stay up late and have bursts of energy later in the day.

1. Set at least two alarms to help you wake up in the morning.
2. Try not to sleep in later than 8 a.m., as sleeping in can make it difficult to go to bed at night.
3. Avoid taking naps, as they can challenge your nighttime sleep.
4. Since mornings may be difficult, use morning time to plan out your day and get organized.
5. Try to schedule your most energy-consuming or challenging activities for the afternoon.
6. It's okay to do your homework or study later in the evening.
7. It's best for you to exercise later in the day, between 6 and 9 p.m.
8. Avoid drinking caffeinated beverages after 2 p.m.
9. Eat a balanced lunch in the afternoon and delay your dinner until around 8 p.m. This will help you sleep better at night.

9 Strategies for Bears

Bears are the most common chronotype, making up about 55 percent of the population. They like to get a full eight hours of sleep and are most productive in the morning and early afternoon.

1. It's okay to hit the snooze button, but be sure to get up by 8 a.m.
2. Since your energy will decline in the afternoon, take a nap (between 20 and 40 minutes).
3. Be sure to take some time in the evening to wind down from your day. This will help you fall asleep faster.
4. Plan and organize your day so that you are doing the most energy-consuming and challenging activities between 10 a.m. and 12 p.m.
5. Your best time to study is late afternoon into early evening.

continued ➡

Overcoming Obstacles

Everyone faces difficult situations and obstacles when trying to achieve their goals, and it can often seem as if life serves up the negatives all at once. Students can't control the surprises that life sets in their way. What they can control is how they prepare for and manage those inevitable challenges. People who successfully set and achieve their goals are those who are able to anticipate, accept, and move beyond disappointment and work through challenges. Though there will always be those things out of our control, generally it is how we choose to move that propels us forward, gets us stuck, or moves us backward.

Michael Phelps, the world's most decorated Olympic athlete, has been open about his challenges with mental health, addiction, and ADHD, and he's a wonderful example to share with students of someone who works hard to overcome the obstacles in his path. One specific story you can share is from his performance at the 2008 Summer Olympics in Beijing, China. The gun sounded to start the final men's 200-meter butterfly. Phelps dove into the pool with his competitors, and his goggles instantly filled with water. In Olympic swimming, races are won in nanoseconds. For Phelps to stop to adjust his goggles would have cost him the race. So he chose to swim on. He not only won the race, but he also broke his own world record.

In post-race interviews, Phelps addressed the challenge he faced and how he was able to overcome it by having prepared himself for almost every obstacle that could get in his way. He'd already practiced swimming without seeing by counting his strokes, so he was able to use this strategy in the moment to achieve his goal of winning another medal.

We're not all Olympic athletes, and we probably don't need to learn how to swim with our eyes closed. But it is important to know how to plan for potential obstacles and adjust when they get in our way. The good news is that these are skills you can develop and ones you can teach your students to help them take charge of their own learning and thrive in school and beyond. Students will feel better (affect) knowing they are prepared to do what needs to be done (behavior), because they have planned to address issues as they arise (cognition).

Strategies for Teachers

Dealing with obstacles, learning from challenges and setbacks, and being prepared for hurdles are life skills that are learned through experience. That's why it's especially important for you to have some strategies to support students as they navigate the challenges of achieving their learning goals. Following are some ways you can support students in anticipating potential obstacles, moving beyond disappointment, and working through challenges.

MODEL HOW YOU APPROACH OBSTACLES

Be open with your students about how you plan for and then deal with the obstacles in your life—both those that are simple and those that are more challenging. For example, perhaps on the way to work, there was major road construction that was going to make you late. You can explain how you dealt with the experience in a positive way and the steps you took to rectify the possible conflicts.

A critical dimension of self-regulation is knowing how to plan for future obstacles. To continue the example above, you might let your students know how you are going to plan for future unexpected road conditions by heading out a little earlier and identifying an alternate route. This way you are leaving yourself a cushion of time and a plan for how to adjust no matter what road conditions arise.

Finally, be sure to also share how you reward yourself when you overcome an obstacle. For example, maybe your planning leads you to make it to work with time to spare. How are you going to reward yourself now that you have extra time? You may take a few minutes to listen to your favorite music, read a few pages from your book, or grab another cup of coffee. Rewarding yourself when you avoid or conquer obstacles shows your students how to do the same.

CREATE A SUPPORTIVE CLASSROOM COMMUNITY

Students need to feel safe making mistakes in order to overcome barriers and achieve their learning goals. In an emotionally supportive classroom, students form effective relationships and can lean on one another for support in navigating challenges in learning. See pages 7–15 on attitude and pages 35–38 in *Self-Regulation in the Classroom: Helping Students Learn How to Learn* for tips on building a safe and supportive classroom community.

INCLUDE ALL LEARNING TYPES

Every person likes to learn differently. But teachers tend to teach the way *they* like to learn. They may miss some learners by not addressing how those students learn best. To ensure you're reaching all learners, be sure to use a variety of teaching methods (see the section on learning preferences on page 21) in your lessons and activities. Having options of learning activities can provide students with avenues for achieving their best. If a student has to work in an area or in a way that is less comfortable for them, consider the hurdles they may encounter. Most likely, the student will need more supports, require more time, and need to put in more effort to achieve the learning goal.

CHECK IN

The best way to ensure that students aren't hitting roadblocks on their way to achieving their learning goals, or to help them navigate such blocks, is to do frequent check-ins. These can be through constructive informal/formal formative assessments, descriptive feedback, or one-on-one coaching. In general, it's best to catch or predict any barriers before they become a problem.

BELIEVE IN EACH STUDENT

We have all heard stories or have our own story about the one teacher who really believed in a student's talents or abilities and how that belief propelled that child on to achieve their goals. Be that teacher who believes in each and every student. Make your belief public in a way that shows students you really care about their success.

BUILD STUDENT RESILIENCE

Many students feel a great deal of academic pressure, either put on them by others or self-imposed. These are some strategies for developing student resilience:

- Help students build social networks with peers and adults who can support them when the going gets tough.
- Focus on effort being the key to success.
- Change happens! Expect and respect it, and model this for students.
- Have students think about what they can control and what they can't control. When they are unable to control a situation, help them stay focused on expecting and respecting the change.
- Teach stress management techniques, like deep breathing, yoga, and relaxation exercises.
- Stay positive! And help students keep a positive attitude as well.
- Focus on the purpose of the learning or activity, rather than the product.
- Guide students to maintain positive self-talk.
- Celebrate with students when they meet a challenge and overcome obstacles.

Visualizing Resilience

Some students need concrete ways to understand the concept of resilience. This activity is a fun way to "see" resilience, to make it more understandable to students. All you need for this activity is a balloon. Have students call out the various challenges in their lives. With each item called, blow into the balloon. As the challenges mount and the balloon gets bigger, ask students what they predict will happen if the challenges keep mounting. (The balloon will eventually burst.) Before it bursts, ask students what items could be removed from the list, and slowly let out small bits of air. At a certain point, show students that eliminating some of the challenges in their lives can actually make them more resilient, like the balloon when it has "just the right amount of air" to make it resistant against outside pressures.

PRAISE EFFORT OVER ACHIEVEMENT

In Dr. Carol Dweck's seminal work *Mindset: The New Psychology of Success* (2006), she expertly lays out how praising effort over perceived ability can benefit learners in developing perseverance and patience in the learning process, in overcoming obstacles, and in achieving their goals. When students meet a challenge or successfully complete a goal, they must know that effort (hard work and dedication) was the key to their success. The process is more important than the product!

Techniques and Tools for Students

All students will experience hurdles on the way to achieving their goals. Knowing how to deal with those inevitable bumps in the road increases their chances of success. Here are some tips to teach students to help them deal with and overcome obstacles.

PLAN AHEAD!

The easiest way to support students in overcoming challenges in learning is to help them plan for obstacles before they arise. Teach these three steps for planning ahead:

1. **Identify potential obstacles.** For example, if students tend to struggle with procrastination, they may anticipate facing this challenge in a long-term project.
2. **Think of ways to avoid obstacles.** Students could combat potential procrastination by breaking a long-term project into smaller chunks and assigning themselves due dates for each chunk along the way.

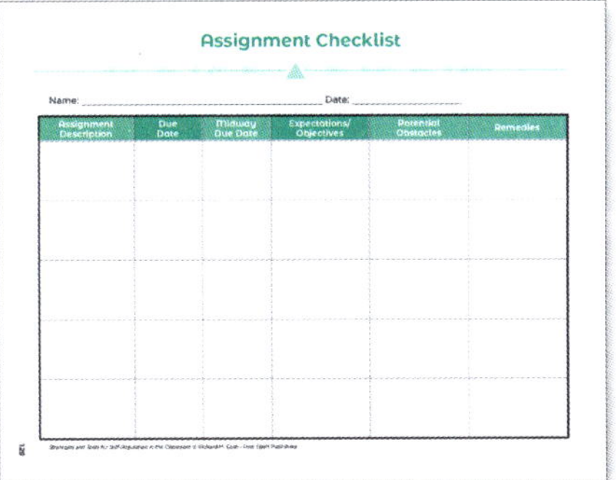

Assignment Checklist

Name: Date:

Assignment Description	Due Date	Midway Due Date	Expectations/ Objectives	Potential Obstacles	Remedies

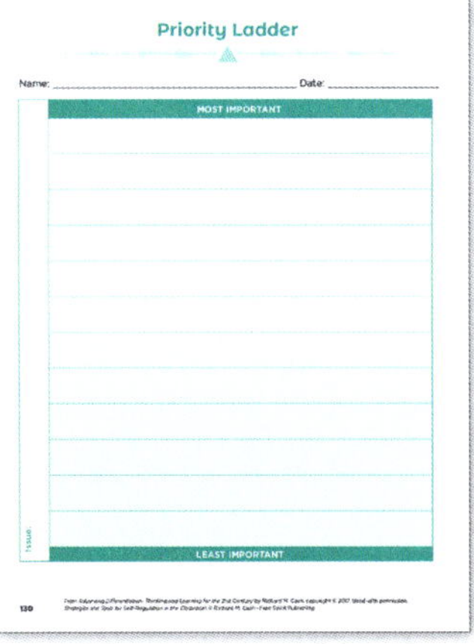

Priority Ladder

Name: Date:

MOST IMPORTANT

LEAST IMPORTANT

3. **Make a plan for how to work through obstacles.** When the inclination to procrastinate hits, students may use the Eisenhower Matrix form on page 128 to help them determine what piece of the project is most crucial right now.

The Assignment Checklist on page 129 can be a useful tool for helping students plan ahead. The Priority Ladder (page 130) is another good tool. It includes a column for predicting possible hurdles and a column for a prepared remedy if the obstacle occurs.

MANAGE MINDSET

Students' abilities to work through obstacles can often depend on how they view those obstacles. Following are a few tips you can share with students for keeping their minds focused on moving forward and achieving their learning goals:

- **Stay positive.** Negative energy can cause students to feel as if their feet are tangled up in weeds. They can set themselves free of those tangles by keeping a positive mindset (see Attitude Counts in part I).
- **Try not to worry about what might happen or what already has happened.** Worrying about something won't change the outcome. It's impossible to plan for and prevent all obstacles. By staying positive and focusing energy on overcoming the problem, students can solve it in a meaningful way.
- **Reframe mistakes as opportunities.** Every mistake, no matter how big, can lead to wonderful outcomes. So teach students to reframe mistakes as learning opportunities. What can they learn from the mistakes they and others make? The ABC questions below can help you guide students toward understanding that mistakes are a chance to learn, grow, improve, and even be creative.
- **Remember that you are not alone.** Sometimes when students are challenged, they can feel as if they're all alone. We know this is rarely true. When challenges start to mount, students can seek out others who know how to deal with issues in a positive way. They can rely on those people, whether they are close friends, peers they sit next to in class, or members of their families or communities. Sharing feelings with trusted people can ease emotional burdens.

ABC Reflections on Obstacles

Affect:

- How do you feel when things don't go well?
- What can you learn about yourself from that feeling?
- How might you be growing, emotionally, as you discover your feelings about making a mistake?

Behavior:

- What did you do that got you to the place you are now?
- What have your learned about yourself from these actions?
- In what ways are you growing as a learner and becoming more creative?

Cognition:

- How did you set your plan and thinking process during this activity/project?
- What have you learned about yourself and your planning methods?
- From this mistake, what did you learn about planning for next time?

MOVE FORWARD

In the story at the top of this section, Michael Phelps didn't take any time or energy to debate his problem or fret about it. He faced the challenge, figured out what to do in the moment, and took charge. Students can do the same. Having the right mindset and a plan already in place can help students feel confident in taking charge of problems, rather than allowing problems to take charge of them. But it's impossible to plan for every possibility. Whether the obstacle a student is facing was planned for or not, you can share these ideas for moving forward.

Focus on the Outcome

When a student meets an obstacle, it can overtake the entire process. Sometimes obstacles are small (such a sibling who won't leave a student alone when they're trying to study), and sometimes they are large (due to their work schedule, a student just doesn't have time to study each night). Teach students to stay focused on what needs to be done and work backward. In the case of a pesky younger sibling, a student might consider asking another family member to keep their sibling occupied while they study. In the case of the work schedule, a student may have to consider eliminating something else from their schedule to gain the time they need to study. Encourage students to ask themselves, "What needs to happen?" and "What do I need to do to get there?" to get them focused on the outcome.

Ask for Help and Accept Support

Asking for help from others, and accepting their support, is not a sign of weakness, and it does not take away from the achievement of a goal. In fact, the smartest, most accomplished people do not do it alone. Remind students that when they seek out help, they are allowing others to shine and contributing to a positive and collaborative learning space. (See pages 110–111 in *Self-Regulation in the Classroom: Helping Students Learn How to Learn.*)

Once students have asked for help, they need to be willing to accept the support. Or maybe they haven't asked for help, but others who care about them can see they are struggling and have offered their assistance. That's great! Encourage students to be open and willing to accept help. And if they'd like to try it on their own a little longer, they can thank the helper for the offer and let the person know that they don't need help at the moment but may take them up on the offer at a later time.

Shrug It Off

How students respond to failure is what's important. Failures and obstacles don't define students, but they are great learning experiences. Thomas Edison famously said, "I never failed. I just found ten thousand ways that didn't work."

Share these ideas for how students can respond:

- Laugh it off.
- Learn from the obstacle.
- Plan ahead for next time.
- Embrace that obstacles happen.
- Stay focused.
- Say, "That didn't work. What's next?"
- Forgive yourself.
- Say, "Just because I hit an obstacle doesn't mean I am an obstacle."

OBSTACLE TOSS

Obstacle Toss is an activity that involves identifying potential or metaphorical barriers and actively addressing them as part of the goal-setting process. Instead of merely acknowledging obstacles as they appear, this approach encourages proactive engagement with potential challenges. This game can help prepare students for setbacks and enhances their problem-solving skills, resilience, and adaptability.

Process:

1. Ask students to each take out a blank sheet of paper and draw a vertical line down the center of it. Have them label the left column "Obstacles." You may need to define for students an obstacle you have met in your life, such as "running out of time to complete a project."
2. Ask them to each think of a specific goal they had for themselves in the past and make a list of the obstacles they encountered in working toward that goal. This is a private list, so encourage them to be as open and honest as possible.
3. Now have them label the right column "Lessons Learned." Across from each obstacle they identified, they should write a lesson they learned from it. Students can write as many lessons as they learned from each obstacle. Be sure to provide them your lesson as an example: "Next time, I will get started on projects sooner and plan for more time."
4. Now, ask students to tear their papers in half. This leaves their lessons in one hand and their obstacles in other hand. Tell them that they now have a choice:
    a. Keep both the obstacles and the lessons.
    b. Keep the obstacles and throw away the lessons.
    c. Keep the lessons and throw away the obstacles.
    d. Throw away both the obstacles and the lessons.
5. If you have time, ask students who have something to throw away to do so.

Extensions:

- **Option A:** After completing the activity, have students do a two- to three-minute quick write about what this experience was like, what they learned from it, or why they chose as they did. Following the quick write, as a class, discuss the choices students made (what they kept and what they threw away) and why, and the lessons they learned.
- **Option B:** In small groups, have each student read their lessons aloud. They just state the lesson, not how they learned it.

PART III:
Monitoring and Adjusting Learning Techniques

Once goals have been set, it's time to work toward achieving those goals. It's time to learn.

Critical to the development of self-regulation for learning is having tools and techniques to make the learning process more efficient and effective. Incorporating these practices into the learning process not only enhances the immediate educational experience but also builds skills and habits that benefit lifelong learning and personal development.

Many things on the learning journey can trip students up. Some students struggle with staying focused in the classroom, others need to learn strategies for taking notes, and still others have a hard time with studying effectively. Some students will possess well-developed learning habits, and others will need lots of support. This section is like an à la carte menu of techniques you can teach students to help them build better habits to monitor and adjust how they are learning.

To determine where students may need support, do an overview of their strengths and limitations with regard to their learning habits. Remember that a student's struggle in one area may not be isolated to just that issue, so it will be helpful for all students to learn and practice a combination of learning strategies.

Listening

Listening is an integral part of human communication that goes beyond the mere act of hearing. It is an active process that involves paying attention, interpreting, and responding to the speaker's message, no matter how you take in information. Listening is about understanding what is being said, and good listening is both active and empathic.

Active listening involves focusing on what someone is saying, and it includes a physical component (think actions like nodding the head or asking questions). Empathic listening involves trying to understand the speaker's feelings and point of view. It promotes a safe and supportive learning environment where each participant feels heard and understood. Both types of listening are necessary to thinking critically, working with complex concepts, and engaging in problem-solving.

Good listening can improve relationships and be a foundation for positive change. Being a good listener is an important quality for learning and success. Good listeners often excel academically because they don't need to ask for clarification, they get to work more quickly, and they know what's expected of them.

Self-regulated learners are good listeners, and they know that listening is an important skill. On the feeling side (affect), they take into account the speaker's emotional responses, as well as their own. This is demonstrated through the overt actions of listening (behavior). By practicing good listening, self-regulated learners can change their minds and sharpen their perspectives (cognition).

This section explores the art of listening and shares strategies to help students become active and empathic listeners.

Strategies for Teachers

Being able to employ both active and empathic listening techniques is an important part of the learning process. The following strategies share ideas you can implement that will support your students' active and empathic listening skills.

SPEAK CLEARLY AND ARTICULATE

This is especially important when teaching academic words (i.e. *analyses*, *concept*, *define*, *express*, *process)* and content-specific vocabulary (i.e. *isotope*, *vertebra*, *axis*, *equation*, *constitution)*. It's best to review these words before a lesson. Provide students with definitions, and even photos, that may help them learn the meaning of the words and recall them later.

GIVE STUDENTS TIME TO DIGEST IMPORTANT POINTS

Here is where the use of "turn and talk" can come in handy. Be sure to provide specifics as to what you want students to discuss:

- Turn to your partner and tell them what you just heard.
- Ask your partner to tell you what was just stated.
- Tell your partner, in your own words, what was just said.
- Along with your partner, draw a picture of what you just heard.
- Share your notes with your partner to see if you agree on what was just stated.

USE VERBAL AND NONVERBAL CUES

The use of cues lets students know that something important is going to be said. Here are a few examples:

Verbal cues

- This next point is important.
- Write this down, just as I say it.
- Listen carefully now.
- Pay close attention to what I'm about to say.

Nonverbal cues

- Pause before the important point.
- Move to a new space in the room to state an important point.
- Hold up your index finger or hand when you're about to say something important.
- Lower your voice or intensify the tone of your voice to indicate importance.

AVOID COLD CALLING

Cold calling is the act of calling on students randomly with no hands up. Be careful with this practice. Shy students and more introverted thinkers may spend the period in fear of being called upon. Students who have difficulty explaining their thinking or who struggle with imposter syndrome may also feel anxious with this practice. And some students lack confidence in themselves.

KEEP YOUR SPACE CLEAR OF AUDIO AND VISUAL NOISE

It can be difficult to pay attention to important information in cluttered or loud environments. Audio noise includes distracting sounds such as background music, multiple conversations going, hammering from a construction site, and traffic sounds or other noises from open windows. Visual noise includes images (projected or posted) that distract from what is being presented, such as a visual that is unrelated to the topic being discussed. When there's too much going on, students may end up paying more attention to the audio and visual noise in the classroom than to what you're trying to teach. Reducing these kinds of distractions ensures that the classroom environment is one that invites students to speak, listen, and be heard.

MODEL GOOD LISTENING

Use the listening tools you are teaching students yourself. Here are a few tips to show students that you are listening to them:

- **Be visibly attentive and interested in what students are saying.** Nod, smile, and look at them when they speak.
- **Don't interrupt when students are trying to get their points across.** Allow them to collect their thoughts, speak their ideas through, and say what they think the way they prefer—even if it's not completely correct or you disagree.
- **Be present when students are speaking.** Put your phone aside, don't look at your notes or computer, and stay focused on the student in front of you.
- **Ask questions to clarify your understanding.** This is also great way to model asking good questions. For more on asking questions, see the Inquiry section on pages 78–84.
- **Restate what students have said, using their own words.** Use phrases like "This sounds like . . ." and "This feels like . . ."

BUILD IN TIME FOR STUDENTS TO TALK

This means you take on the role of listener. Offer students appealing topics that are interesting to discuss. Be the facilitator of the conversation and interject only to keep the discussion moving and on topic.

GET TO KNOW STUDENTS

By learning what students are interested in, what they do for fun, and what is happening in their lives, you demonstrate the qualities of a good listener and show that you care about who they are.

LISTEN MORE THAN YOU SPEAK

Typically, at the beginning of the school year, teachers talk about 80 percent of the time and students talk about 20 percent of the time. As the year progresses, your goal should be for you to listen 80 percent of the time to allow students frequent opportunities to speak.

WAIT

One of the qualities of a good listener is not rushing others' thoughts. Being patient and waiting when asking students to speak shows that you are interested in and ready to hear what they have to say. There are two types of wait time:

- Wait time #1: Before asking students to respond to a question, allow at least ten seconds for students to process their ideas and answers.
- Wait time #2: After students have answered questions, ask them to pause and think for at least ten seconds about which answers they heard were the most reasonable, which answers they would add to, which answers were less grounded in evidence, and so on.

Techniques and Tools for Students

The world is a noisy place! Good listeners have the ability to break through the noise to hear what's being said and to understand what's being communicated through tone of voice and body language. Teach students the following tools and techniques to improve their active and empathic listening skills.

ELIMINATE DISTRACTIONS

This might include turning devices off or upside down so the screen can't be seen, closing laptops, and silencing notifications. Ask students to avoid looking at their watches or the clock when listening to others, as this may send a nonverbal message that they don't care about what is being said.

TRY NOT TO INTERRUPT

Sometimes it may take a person time to form their thoughts or elaborate on what they mean. Interruptions can be frustrating and cause the speaker to lose track of what they were saying. Pausing and allowing for a bit of silence can benefit the speaker *and* the listener—giving each person time to process.

If students aren't sure what someone is saying, such as when a person is speaking too quickly or too quietly, politely asking the speaker to slow down, speak up, or repeat what they just said can help students better grasp the speaker's meaning.

LOOK AT THE SPEAKER

Looking at the person speaking helps students fully understand what someone is saying and pick up on nonverbal communication, such as when the speaker may be trying to be funny, sarcastic, or forceful in their point of view. Research by Albert Mehrabian in the 1960s suggests the breakdown is 55 percent body language, 38 percent tone of voice, and 7 percent the actual words spoken (Thompson 2011). This suggests that a total of 93 percent of human communication is nonverbal. Therefore, looking at the speaker to get a complete understanding of their message is important.

To help students better understand nonverbal communication, share the following nine ways humans communicate without words:

1. **Body language.** How we position our bodies communicates our feelings, such as standing back in fear, leaning forward in curiosity, or folding our arms in disbelief.
2. **Movement.** How we use our arms and legs also communicates how we feel, such as walking slowly in apprehension, fidgeting out of restlessness, or sitting due to being uncomfortable.
3. **Posture.** The way we stand can communicate exhaustion, inquisitiveness, or our general disposition.
4. **Gestures.** These can vary widely across cultures and communities, but the way we move our fingers, arms, and legs to make a point can have both intended and unintended implications. For example, actions such as nodding can communicate agreement, waving arms can communicate wanting attention, and shrugging can communicate not understanding what is being said.
5. **Space.** How close we are to the speaker/listener and whether we place objects between us (such as a lectern, table, or partition) can communicate levels of authority, fear, or reluctance to relate to an audience.
6. **Paralanguage.** Speech intonation, pitch, speed, and other non-lexical noises impact the message the listener hears. Non-lexicals are not words. They are sounds or utterances that contribute to what the listener hears, such as *um*, *uh*, or vocalizations like coughs or grunts. Paralanguage such as a high pitch or quick speech can communicate that you are nervous. Using a lot of non-lexicals may communicate that you are not sure of what you are saying or that you are unprepared.
7. **Facial expression** How we move our eyebrows, eyes, and other facial muscles can communicate our feelings and can impact how our words (or reactions) are received. For example, raised eyebrows can communicate judgment, disbelief, or surprise.
8. **Eye contact.** Where and at whom we look when we speak affects how our listeners receive our message. If you avoid eye contact with your audience, this may communicate you are unsure of your message. If you are making a statement and looking directly at one person, that can be perceived as threatening. Try to distribute your eye contact around the room when speaking to a group of people. A trick used by actors is to look at the audience's foreheads, rather than directly into their eyes. This little tip will make you, the speaker more comfortable, and can help listeners feel less intimidated.
9. **Touch.** When we touch someone while we are speaking to them, say on the shoulder or hand, this can communicate support, comfort, friendship, and intimacy. However, touch between strangers or unknown persons should be used in a very limited fashion so as to not offend or invade personal space.

USE INTERJECTIONS

Teach students appropriate and positive interjections they can use to show someone they are engaged in listening and following along. Interjections are utterances that lack grammatical connections, such as words or phrases of exclamation (wow! interesting!) or that express some emotion (oh, okay, exciting).

SUSPEND JUDGMENT

When listening, it is important to allow the speaker to say what they have to say, even if we don't agree with their ideas. Advise students not to plan their responses while they are listening, as this may cause them to miss important points or errors in the speaker's thinking process. They should listen the whole time someone is speaking, collect their thoughts, and then offer their disagreement with or challenge to what was said.

LISTEN FOR REPEATED WORDS

Repetition can indicate that a word or idea has special meaning or is important to the subject matter. Repeated words are also used to form a rhythm to help a speaker's audience remember a message. When taking notes during a lesson or lecture, students can write down the repeated words for future reference. If students are not sure of a word's meaning, they can note the unknown word and look it up later.

ASK CLARIFYING QUESTIONS

Asking good questions of a speaker shows attentiveness and demonstrates thoughtful scholarship. Well-formed questions restate the key point made by the speaker, are nonthreatening (meaning they do not provoke an emotional response), and invite a thoughtful reply. Good questions are often open ended. Open-ended questions allow the speaker an opportunity to clarify or adjust verbiage, without feeling threatened in a "gotcha" moment. Additionally, open-ended questions show the listener's curiosity and respect for the speaker.

Here are examples of clarifying questions:

- Would you provide me with examples of what you are saying?
- Would you tell me more about that?
- Where might I find additional information?
- How can I use what you are saying in the future?
- Is what you're saying just to help me understand your position, or are you trying to convince me to change my position?
- Would you clarify what XYZ means?
- How might this information connect to what we have learned?
- Can you relate what you are saying to something we have studied?

RESTATE WHAT WAS SAID

There are several ways to help students learn how to restate what they have heard. This is not about students repeating exactly what was said, but about using their own words. Restating assists students in getting a fuller understanding of what someone is telling them. Teach these restating starters:

- Let me see if I have this correct . . .
- So what you are saying is . . .
- In other words, . . .
- Here is what I heard . . .
- To put it another way . . .
- In essence, you are saying . . .

CHECK FOR UNDERSTANDING

Providing students with starter sentences or question cues they can use to check their understanding can help them refine this skill. These types of questions or statements are different from clarifying questions, because they help the listener understand the *meaning* behind a speaker's words. Teaching students to check their understanding puts the listening responsibility on them and can be much more effective than you just asking if they understand. Cues include the following:

- What I hear you saying is . . .
- Do you mean . . . ?
- Correct me if I'm wrong . . .
- In essence, you're saying . . .
- So, in your opinion . . .
- To paraphrase . . .
- To simplify what I heard . . .

ACTIVE LISTENING

Seeing nonverbal communication and listening techniques in action can help students better understand how to use them. In this activity, students will watch a video and observe how the subjects are using active and empathic listening techniques, as well as nonverbal communication. For activities that require students to practice listening to complete a task, see the creative dramatics on pages 12–15.

Process:

1. Select a short video clip for students to view. Be sure to select a video that is age appropriate.
2. Tell students to look for the following things when viewing the video clip:
   - one or two of the nine nonverbal communication methods
   - successful listening techniques
   - unsuccessful listening techniques
   - outcome of the use of or lack of use of listening skills
3. Discuss with students what they observed, asking questions such as these:
   - What did you see? What did you hear?
   - How did each person in the video use listening techniques?
   - What were the outcomes based on the listening techniques?
   - How might the people in the video have changed their strategy?
   - Why would the change be better/worse?
   - How can you apply this to your life?
   - Has something like this happened to you?
   - What will you do next time you encounter a situation such as this?

Note-Taking

Note-taking is one of the most common study practices in education. Whether they're working in elementary, secondary, or higher education, educators often expect students to be able to keep notes on what is taught during class time. However, students may not know how to take accurate notes or how to use the notes they do take effectively. Additionally, not all note-taking is created equal—some techniques are more helpful than others, leading to various degrees of success.

Taking notes is a difficult and complex process, and one that must be learned. Even when students know how to take notes, research shows that they only capture between 25 and 50 percent of the important information (Willingham 2023). This is why it's essential to teach various note-taking methods and strategies. Learning to take accurate notes can greatly improve students' memories and, ultimately, their academic performance.

Being a good note-taker requires being a good listener first and foremost. Students need to know what to take notes on, which means being able to hear and comprehend the information that is being delivered. (If this is where your students are getting stuck, you may want to focus on teaching strategies for active and empathic listening first. See pages 63–68.)

Note-taking requires the use of the three dimensions of self-regulation for learning. It's the act of taking notes (behavior) that helps with understanding of the content (cognition). This in turn can help students feel a sense of success and pride in the classroom (affect).

Based on research, this section spells out several useful note-taking techniques. Since note-taking is an interactive exchange between teacher and students, also included are ideas you can use to ensure that students are taking the best notes possible.

Strategies for Teachers

Taking notes requires students to listen, think, write, draw, and document all at once. It's a very complex process. It also requires them to know which system of note-taking to use, depending on the content or topic, the format of the information being delivered, and the way *they* retain information best. This is why note-taking can often be faulty, ineffective, and time consuming. However, through strategic instruction you can teach students how to do a better job capturing important information.

It will take time in the beginning to teach students how to take good notes, but it is time well spent. Following are some tips for supporting students in learning this skill.

START SMALL

Don't overwhelm your students with too much information as they're learning to take notes. Start with a small amount of information and try to make note-taking a fun experience.

With younger students, start with content students know. For example, they could take notes on the appearance and taste of an apple. Gradually move to more information, ensuring students are grasping the need to take notes.

With intermediate students, as with younger students, start by using content they know. Consider doing note-taking as a class and have students share with partners how they documented the information. Allow them to correct or improve each other's notes.

Many secondary students may have never been taught how to take notes and, therefore, take inaccurate or distracting notes. To teach note-taking, start with a simple method using content they know and move up to more complex styles, such as Cornell Notes (page 72) or Outlining (page 75).

START EARLY

Students are never too young to begin learning how to take notes. With younger students, the focus of note-taking should be on identifying key points, words, or phrases. At first it is okay for students to copy the teacher's exact words or phrases, but you will want to encourage them toward writing their own thoughts in their own words. Here are a few methods to teach note-taking to younger students:

- **Drawings.** Since younger students may not possess sufficient written language yet, having them draw as their first form of note-taking can help them create memories of important details. To practice, have students listen to a short passage from a picture book or video. Tell them to draw one thing they remember from what they just heard or saw. Students share their ideas with partners or the entire class.
- **Add a word/simple sentence.** Take drawn notes to the next level by having students add a word, then a simple sentence to their drawings. Check out the Note-Taking with Pictures and Words form on page 144 for an outline students can use.
- **Key points.** This moves students toward writing notes rather than drawing pictures. The Note-Taking Organizer form on page 145 provides an outline students can use. In it, there are specific boxes for particular bits of information. This will help students begin to organize their thinking and lead to better note-taking in subsequent grade levels. You can also use this outline without prescribed labels in the boxes. As students mature in their note-taking skills, they can decide labels on their own.
- **Begin teaching the Five R's of Note-Taking (page 72).** Start younger students with Record and Review. Add Reduce, Recite, and Reflect as students become confident in their skills.

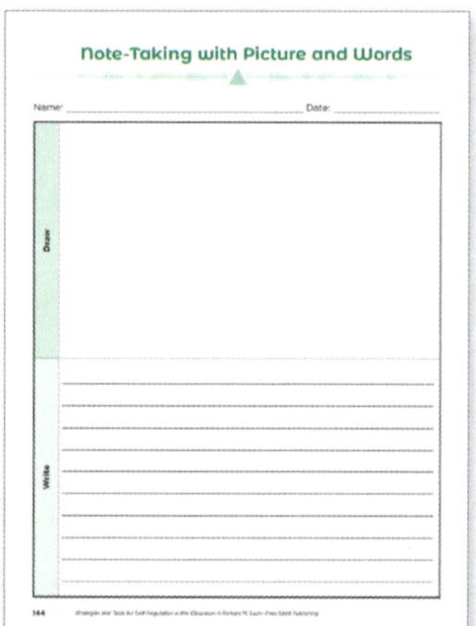
Note-Taking with Picture and Words

Name: ________ Date: ________

Draw

Write

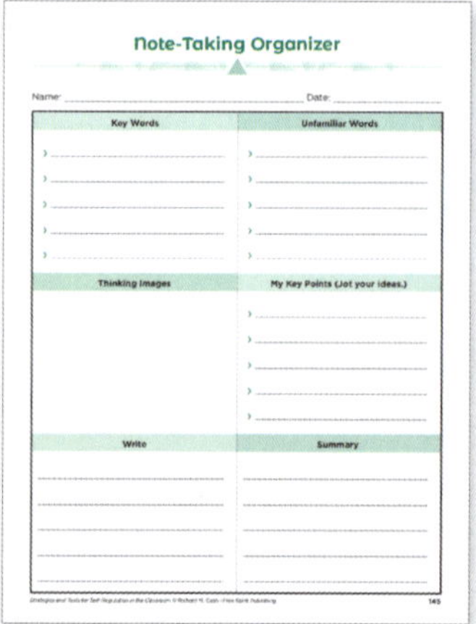
Note-Taking Organizer

Name: ________ Date: ________

Key Words	Unfamiliar Words
Thinking Images	My Key Points (Jot your ideas.)
Write	Summary

TEACH NOTE-TAKING METHODS

Several note-taking methods are covered in the techniques and tools for students below. To teach students a note-taking method, have them listen, read, and/or observe first before taking notes. Repeat the lecture, reading, or observation, having students take notes on the second run. Then they share with partners what they noted and work together to adjust or add to their notes. You can also have them practice a method by taking notes on a scene from a well-known movie or show using the method. Show the scene first without asking students to take notes, then replay the scene while students take notes.

TEACH THE ART OF PARAPHRASING

Note-taking is not about writing everything that was heard, read, or observed. It's about documenting information in one's own words (the What? So What? Now What? method on page 73 works well for teaching paraphrasing, as does the Gist Method below).

Gist Method

The Gist Method is an excellent way to build student comprehension, as well as students' paraphrasing and summarizing skills.

1. Have students preview an unfamiliar text. Direct them to focus on the headings, subheadings, and images like charts, graphs, and pictures.
2. Ask students to each create a list of words or phrases from the text. Help them focus on key vocabulary words. This will help them gain a greater understanding of the entire text.
3. Students reread the text.
4. After they've read the text a second time, have students flip over the text so they are unable to see it. Ask them to write down in twenty words or fewer the "gist" of what they read.

HIGHLIGHT IMPORTANT INFORMATION

Repeat statements or items you want students to remember—even writing them down so students can see what you believe to be the important points. Pause frequently, especially after you've shared key information, so students can catch up on what they are documenting and check to see if they got their information correct.

If you're presenting slides or visuals, try to keep the information on your visuals limited and focused on key details. Too much information will be confusing and distract from the key points. Limit slides to a few words and graphics.

DEMONSTRATE HOW YOU TAKE NOTES

You can do this using a document camera or smartboard so students can see your process. Use a scene from a movie or television program as an example. Be sure to talk through your thought process as you go.

MAKE NOTE-TAKING A TEAM SPORT

The more ears and eyes on a topic, the better. Notes can be shared, compared, and evaluated by others. This is a great way to ensure that students haven't missed important details. If you find that most students missed the highlights or key points, it may be that your instruction needs to be adjusted.

Techniques and Tools for Students

Most students need to be directly taught how to take notes. Some will prefer straightforward methods, such as Outlining, while others will prefer a more abstract way of gathering information, such as Concept Mapping. Following are several methods students can use to take notes.

FIVE R'S OF NOTE-TAKING

Based on work by Cornell University's Walter Pauk (1989), the father of Cornell Notes, here are five R's for effective note-taking. These five R's are useful no matter the note-taking method being used. They also correspond to how the brain remembers information.

1. **Record.** During class time, students listen carefully and jot down important points they hear. The goal is to note the essence of the ideas and not to write down exactly what they heard, read, or observed. Students should do their best to write clearly and legibly so that when they return to the information, they know what was being recorded.
2. **Reduce.** Soon after students have taken their original notes, they write a summary of the ideas and information they gained. This summary should include important points and vocabulary, clarify any words or points students may not feel sure they know, and make connections between ideas and words. These will become students' cue words to help them remember the information. This step is helpful in strengthening memory and distributes preparation for exams over the course of learning.
3. **Recite.** Students take time to go over their notes and then paraphrase the main points and ideas out loud in their own words, without looking at their notes. This may seem like an odd step, but it can help students retain information by giving their own voices to their notes.
4. **Reflect.** This is when students think about their notes. They might ask themselves questions or create analogies for what they are studying. For example, if students are studying photosynthesis, they might reflect that photosynthesis is like going to the store to stock up on food to eat later in the week.
5. **Review.** It is generally best for students to distribute their study over the entire period of learning something new. Each day, they can spend a few minutes reviewing their notes, highlighting key points and words. "Cramming" before a test is a generally ineffective learning strategy and should be avoided!

NOTE-TAKING METHODS

The following sections outline five note-taking methods students can use throughout their school careers and beyond. To teach a method, first demonstrate it for students. Have students copy the method as you demonstrate. Provide them opportunities to practice the method, and, as they feel more comfortable with it, encourage them to adjust the method to fit their needs. After students have practiced and refined a few methods, they can make their own decisions as to which method they prefer. They may even combine methods as they become more independent note-takers.

It is best to develop note-taking skills by practicing all the methods throughout the elementary and middle school years. Then, when students get to high school, they can choose the style and method that fits the content area and their personal preferences. Of course, it's never too late to learn good note-taking strategies, so you can certainly review and teach these methods to older students. As you teach note-taking, start with simple methods and move to more complex ones as students mature and develop their skills. Following are five simple-to-complex methods.

Cornell Notes

One of the most popular note-taking systems is Cornell Notes. Developed by Professor Walter Pauk from Cornell University (Pauk and Owens 2010), this note-taking method offers students several ways to document information from lectures, readings, videos, online text, or class discussions. Once students have become familiar with the system, they should modify the format to fit their needs. The benefit of Cornell Notes is that it allows students to engage their brains in a few different ways so as to make the notes more meaningful and memorable.

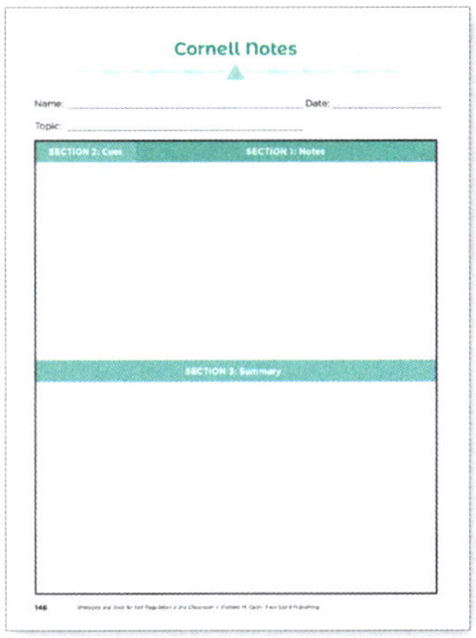

Cornell Notes are divided into three sections. An outline students can use is on page 146.

1. **Notes.** In this section, students write notes about what they hear, read, or view. They shouldn't write everything verbatim, as that defeats the purpose of taking notes. Teach students to use abbreviations or symbols to get down the gist of the information. The notes section can also include quotes from texts, diagrams or pictures, equations and formulas, and other information that is stressed, repeated, or written on the board.
2. **Cues.** When first teaching this method, guide students to use the Cues section after they have taken notes. This section can be used to jot questions, identify points of interest, clarify information, note what needs to be developed, or create images or symbols to help remember important points. Once students have become more proficient with the method, they can use the Cues section *during* note-taking to ask questions as they arise, analyze information, or focus on information that needs attention. Using the Cues section during note-taking can help students stay attentive to the information being presented through critical reasoning and questioning.
3. **Summary.** The famous educational philosopher John Dewey (1910) believed that people do not necessarily learn from experience. Rather, Dewey claimed that learning happens through reflecting on experiences. Reflection is an extremely important phase in the learning process. This phase must not be missed or skipped, no matter how rushed the period may feel. Teach students that if there is not enough time during the class session for this section, they should return to it soon after class. The Summary section is so important because it is the place where students note what they have learned during the period. It's important to distill the information, make connections to other information or topics, and refine or put into their own words what they heard, read, viewed, or discussed.

What? So What? Now What?

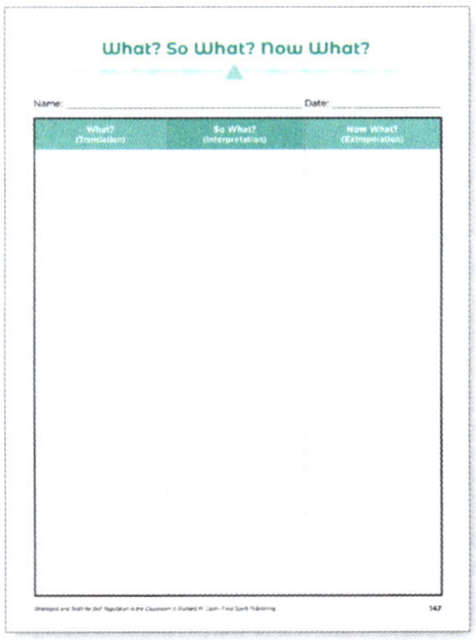

This three-column note-taking method is a great way to involve students in restating information in their own words to show they understand what they heard, read, or discussed. An outline students can use is on page 147.

- **What? (Translation).** In this column students translate information into their own words, summarizing the meaning. This is a basic recall level, which allows students to listen and then write. This is also the section where students can take direct notes during the lesson, reading, or class discussion.
- **So What? (Interpretation).** This column is the next level of comprehension: interpreting the meaningfulness of the information. This means students must make personal connections to the information or put it into the context of the entire topic of study. Students can paraphrase, restate, or summarize the information in a personally meaningful way. This kind of open-endedness forces students to inductively reason through the content.
- **Now What? (Extrapolation).** The final column is for students to extrapolate. Extrapolating involves extending the information into the future—making predictions, estimations,

assumptions, or conclusions based on what came before. Students use this column to hypothesize or theorize how things will change or what could happen. Students also look for trends that may continue or results that can be predicted.

Spider Diagram

This note-taking method helps students put information in strands. It is most effective when taking notes from a text or lecture filled with facts. In the example below, you can see how this method is helpful in organizing information around a specific topic. A reproducible for students can be found on page 148.

Figure 7: Spider Diagram Example

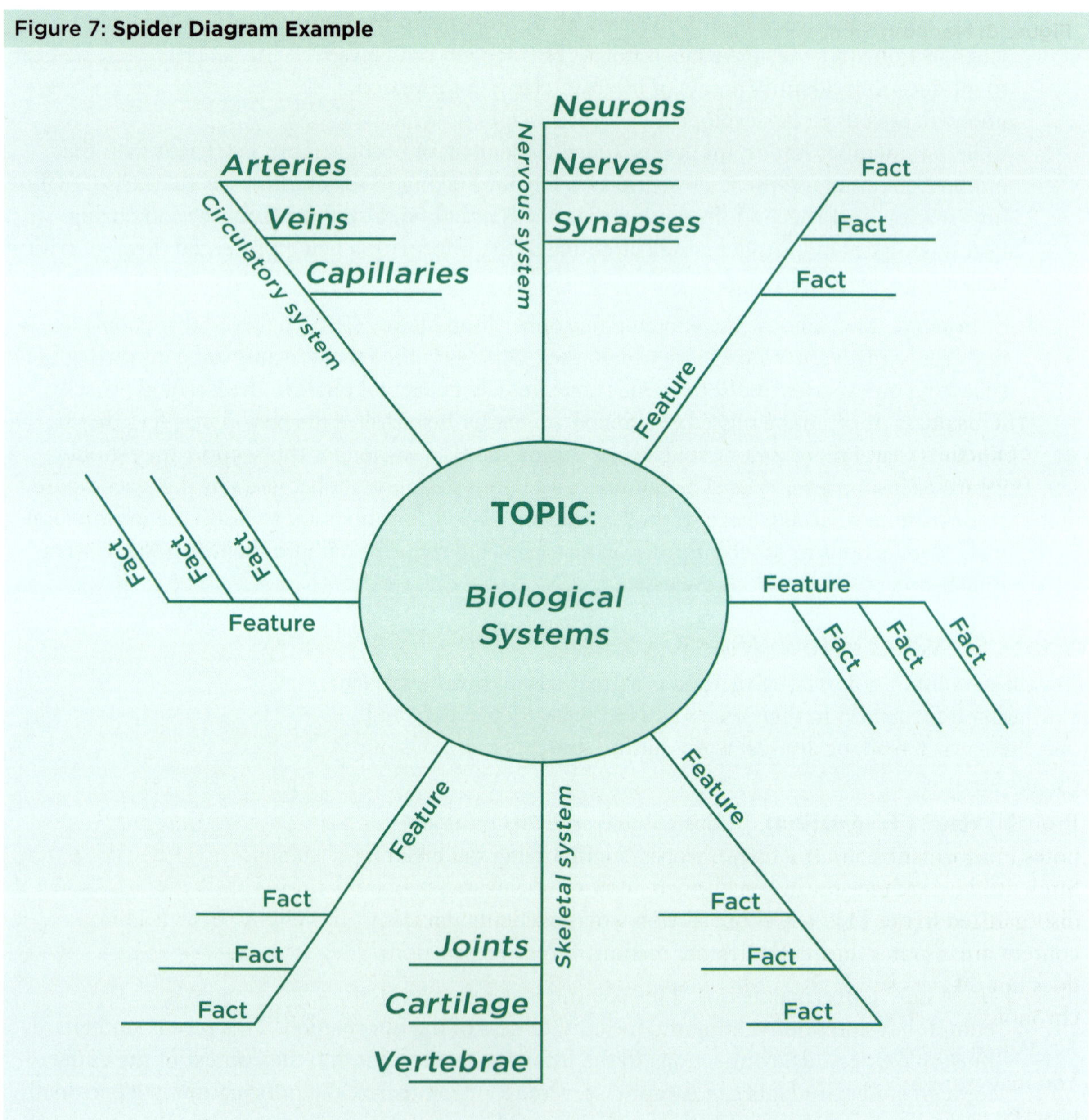

Mapping

Mapping is a note-taking method that helps students make connections between bits of information within a topic. It's a good strategy for visually oriented learners. In the example below, the main topic is in the large central bubble. As students take in information, they make smaller bubbles that connect to and support the bigger idea. The lines between bubbles should link back to the big idea.

Younger students might draw pictures or place images in the bubbles to help them remember the connections between the main topic and the supporting details. Older students can use the mapping strategy to separate content into different categories for more sophisticated note-taking. By reviewing the different categories, students will recognize cause-and-effect connections between them.

Figure 8: **Mapping Example**

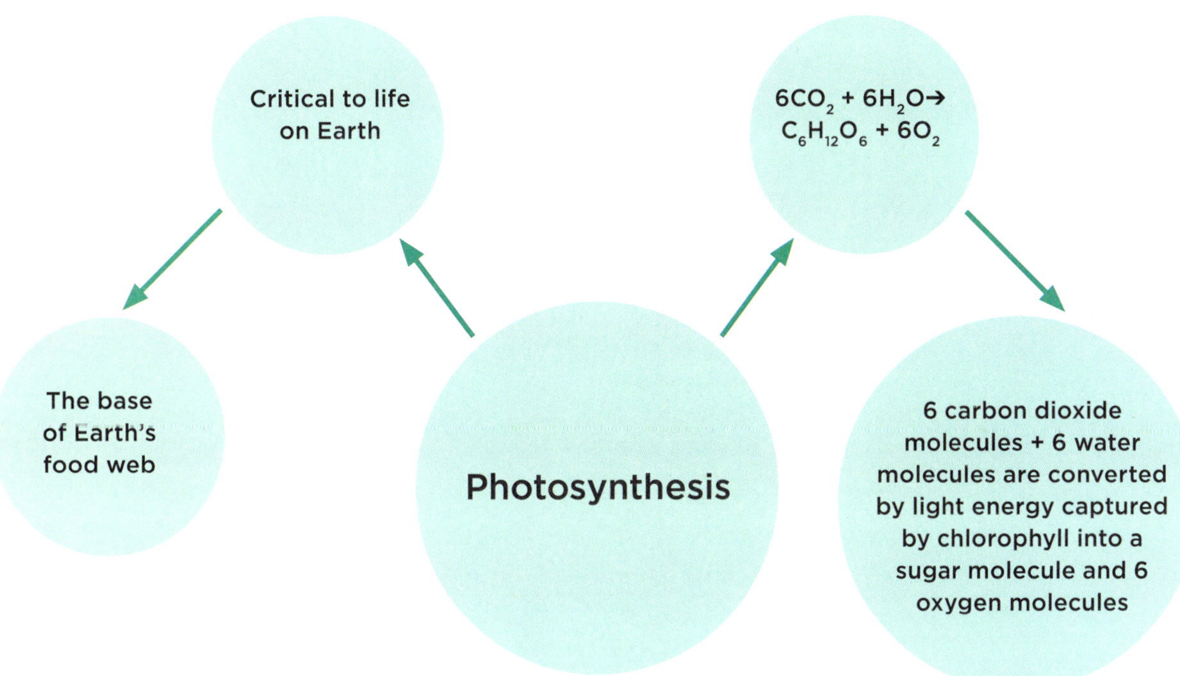

Outlining

Probably one of the most used, and most often misused, note-taking methods is outlining. Taking notes in an organized outline requires prior knowledge of the hierarchy embedded within the content. Students who are new to the information, who have little background knowledge, or who are generally disorganized in the way they think may find that outlining doesn't work well for them. Additionally, in content areas such as mathematics and chemistry that are loaded with equations and graphs, outlining does not offer a useful way to organize information. For content areas with a great deal of verbiage and chronology, such as literature and history, outlining can work well.

When teaching students how to outline, it is best to begin with an example for them to follow. You may want to give them a partial outline, having them fill in the blanks as they read, listen, and/or observe. Note on the example outline how the main ideas are farthest to the left and subpoints to the main ideas are indented to the right. Explain to students that the less important the information is, the farther to the right it moves.

Figure 9: Outlining Example

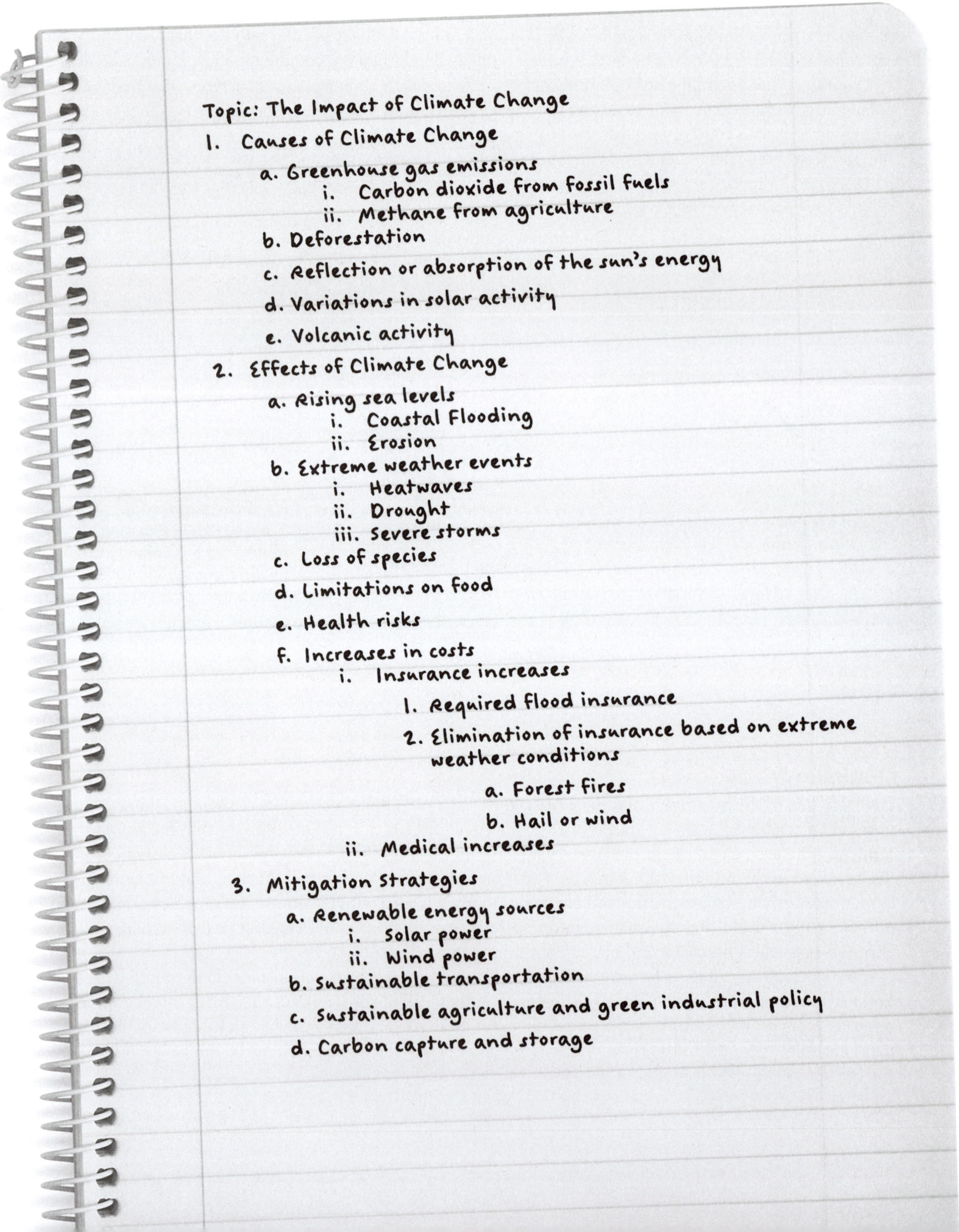

Topic: The Impact of Climate Change

1. Causes of Climate Change
    - a. Greenhouse gas emissions
        - i. Carbon dioxide from fossil fuels
        - ii. Methane from agriculture
    - b. Deforestation
    - c. Reflection or absorption of the sun's energy
    - d. Variations in solar activity
    - e. Volcanic activity
2. Effects of Climate Change
    - a. Rising sea levels
        - i. Coastal Flooding
        - ii. Erosion
    - b. Extreme weather events
        - i. Heatwaves
        - ii. Drought
        - iii. Severe storms
    - c. Loss of species
    - d. Limitations on food
    - e. Health risks
    - f. Increases in costs
        - i. Insurance increases
            - 1. Required flood insurance
            - 2. Elimination of insurance based on extreme weather conditions
                - a. Forest fires
                - b. Hail or wind
        - ii. Medical increases
3. Mitigation Strategies
    - a. Renewable energy sources
        - i. Solar power
        - ii. Wind power
    - b. Sustainable transportation
    - c. Sustainable agriculture and green industrial policy
    - d. Carbon capture and storage

MORE TIPS FOR NOTE-TAKING

Share these additional note-taking tips with students.

- **Handwrite notes.** Though writing notes by hand can be laborious, the process allows students to practice taking notes in many different ways, without the restrictions of linear typing. Additionally, neuroscience informs us that writing by hand uses more regions of the brain, thus putting information into a broader area for memory and retention (Marano et al. 2025).
- **Use "shorthand" notes.** Shorthand notes include abbreviations or symbols that help students recall the longer words or the relationships between ideas. Common shorthand symbols and abbreviations include the following:
  - because: b/c
  - years: yrs
  - with: w/
  - without: w/o
  - amount: amt
  - minimum: min
  - maximum: max
  - between: b/w
  - more than: >
  - less than: <
  - the same as: =
  - different from: ≠
- **Review and evaluate notes soon after creating them.** Have students share their notes with partners, offering each other tips, corrections, adjustments, and additions.
- **Minimize distractions.** Good note-taking requires students to pay attention to important information. Share the tipsheet for minimizing distractions on page 150 with students. And have students reflect on their affect, behavior, and cognition as they think through ways to avoid distractions.

Tips for Avoiding Distractions

RE-CREATING NOTES

Re-creating the day's notes at home (without referring to the original notes) can signal to students what they retained in memory and where they might need to focus their study efforts. If you review the notes students return to class with, you will able to see where your instruction was solid and what items need to be retaught.

Process:

1. After a class period where students took notes, students leave their notes at school.
2. At home that night, students re-create their notes from the class period.
3. The next day, students compare the notes they took during class with the notes they constructed at home.
4. After reviewing their own notes, students work with a peer to compare notes, both those that were taken during class time and those constructed at home.

Inquiry

Inquiry is the act of asking questions to gain knowledge, support ideas, define what is known or unknown, and so on. In today's world, effective inquiry is a crucial learning technique. Asking questions allows students to dig deeper into information, seek out truth, eliminate bias, combat disinformation, and think critically.

It's been said that there are no "stupid" questions. While that may be true, educators also know that sometimes a question is asked in an attempt to get the group off topic or as a way to show off. Perhaps, for instance, while discussing the causes and effects of the French Revolution, a student asks, "Who invented French fries?" or "Many believe Napolean to be of short stature, was this just a way to discredit his military prowess?" While these questions may not be "stupid," they can be annoying and take away valuable class time for more serious kinds of questions. In other cases, students won't ask questions because "they (1) 'don't want to be annoying,' (2) 'don't want to look stupid,' or (3) 'are shy'" (Willingham 2023, 21).

Knowing how to ask questions can greatly improve self-regulation for learning. Thinking about good questions, furthering knowledge, and deepening understanding is the cognitive domain. Knowing when and how to ask questions is behavioral. Improving retention of information, transferring knowledge, and being engaged increases the feelings (affect) of success and empowerment.

Asking effective questions is such an important part of monitoring and adjusting learning. Questioning helps students refine their thinking, pursue topics of interest, and monitor their understanding of content. This section is devoted to helping students learn how to ask good questions and how to ask for help. The tools and techniques described here will empower students to overcome the fear of others' disapproval and learned helplessness.

Strategies for Teachers

Teaching students how to ask good questions has far-reaching benefits. From fostering critical thinking and active learning to enhancing communication skills and stimulating curiosity, the ability to ask insightful questions is essential for intellectual and personal growth. By prioritizing this skill, educators can create engaging, inclusive, and dynamic learning environments that prepare students for future success and lifelong learning.

ASK VARIOUS LEVELS OF QUESTIONS

When you use multiple levels of questions, you challenge students to think in new ways. The Four Levels of Questions on page 79 (Heacox and Cash 2020) is a method to increase sophistication in students' thinking, from recalling information (factual and convergent) to creating new knowledge (divergent) and defending a claim (analytical).

Part of teaching inquiry skills is teaching students not only how to answer questions at each of the four levels, including providing evidence to support their answers at the divergent and analysis levels, but also how to identify questions at the four levels and how to ask their own questions at each level. Here are ways to get students practicing asking and answering questions at the four levels:

- **Home study.** Have students create questions (as well as answers) at each of the four levels. To differentiate the assignment, students who need the most support create and answer one factual and one convergent question, as well as one divergent or one analytical question. More advanced questioners create and answer one divergent and one analytical question, as well as one factual or one convergent question. As a review or preparation for an assessment, students share their questions with small groups or study buddies to elicit answers.

› **Formative or summative assessment.** Having students create and answer questions at the four levels is a great strategy for assessment. Often, students will create more elaborate and tougher questions than the text provides or the teacher would create.

› **Station rotation.** Use the four levels of questions in a station rotation or as separate stations. For example, if using one station, the first set of students creates the four different kinds of questions (and creates an answer key). During the next rotation, another group answers the questions, using the answer key to check their work. That group then creates a new set of questions and an answer key for the next group. Do this until all students have created and answered the four types of questions.

Four Levels of Questions

1. **Factual questions** are closed-ended questions that seek factual answers that are either right or wrong. These questions are verifiable through text and form the foundation in a content area. *Example: Who is the main character?*
2. **Convergent questions** are questions that ask for lists of verifiable information and are often closed-ended. The information needed to answer these types of questions can also be found in the text, but reaching a conclusion will require a level of interpretation, inference, and evaluation. There is usually more than one answer. *Example: What are various ways to find the product of 34 x 96?*
3. **Divergent questions** are questions that open up differing lines of thought, seek creative and imaginative solutions, and likely have multiple answers. When forming answers at this level, students must have a solid knowledge base, which allows them to project, use intuition, and draw on their imagination to come up with new ideas or solutions. *Example: What would happen if there were no rain this summer?*
4. **Analytical questions** are questions that require more thought than is required for simple answers and involve deeper logic and interpretation. As the name states, these questions are analytical in nature and seek to connect content areas, consider various causes and effects, are open-ended, and oftentimes use *why. Example: Why might civilizations rise and/or fall?*

USE QUESTIONING FREQUENTLY

Incorporate questioning throughout the entire learning process. Be sure to vary the types of questions you ask, when you ask them, and how students should respond to them.

In general, try to spend more time on higher-cognitive-level questions (*how* and *why)* and less time on lower-cognitive-level questions (*who, what, when, where).* While lower-cognitive-level questions are important for ensuring students know information, those types of questions do not check for understanding. Understanding is the ability to transfer information from one context to another. *How* and *why* questions require students to make those connections.

When asking students to answer questions, be sure to leave them time to plan their answers, think through difficult information, and speak through their reasoning. See page 65 for more on wait time.

ENCOURAGE CRITICAL THINKING

One of the most essential tools needed in today's world is critical reasoning. To think this way, one must analyze information and question its validity. The overwhelming nature of information access via technology has increased the amount of disinformation and misinformation in the world. Now with the rise of artificial intelligence (AI), information is even more susceptible to being inaccurate, untrue, fake, or simply wrong.

Being able to analyze and evaluate information requires the thinker to ask the right questions, seek greater understanding of where the information originated, and verify context and content. Below are seven critical questioning strategies to use every day. You can find more on these strategies in my book *Advancing Differentiation: Thinking and Learning for the 21st Century* (2017).

Seven Critical-Questioning Strategies

1. **Analogy.** These kinds of questions help students with transforming information from one context to another. *Example: How is a car (concrete) like an idea (abstract)? Provide examples to support your response.*
2. **Analysis of point of view.** These questions help students determine the validity or foundation of the information they're learning. *Example: How can you detect bias in an editorial writer's commentaries? Support your answer with text.*
3. **Complete an incomplete.** These questions require students to draw on prior knowledge and other resources to problem-solve. *Example: Mars is NASA's next frontier. Who do you think will be selected to make the first journey? Support your answer with reasoned evidence.*
4. **Webbing.** This helps students see the ripple effect of an issue or conflict. It can also be used as a tool to uncover and analyze interrelated information. *Example: Graphically represent the effects alternative energy sources have on the United States and international economies. Be sure to support your reasoning with evidence.*
5. **Hypothetical thinking.** These kinds of questions require students to use logical reasoning and abstract thinking to investigate problems. *Example: What if overland trucking were banned? What effect would this have on the US economy? Support your answer with evidence.*
6. **Reversal of thinking.** These questions can stimulate new thinking when a student gets stuck by reframing the information and looking at a problem from a new point of view. *Example: From the perspective of a parent, what are the most important factors to consider when sending your child to school? Support your response with evidence.*
7. **Application of different symbol systems.** This asks students to translate information into a new form, which is especially effective for students who process information visually. *Example: Draw a picture without words or numbers that represents your understanding of linear equations.*

ASK FOLLOW-UP QUESTIONS

To encourage students to clarify their answers and thinking, ask follow-up questions. Here are a few helpful prompts:

- Tell me more.
- Please add to that answer.
- Where did you find that information?
- How can you explain it in a different way?
- Please provide an example.
- What else can be added to that information?

Techniques and Tools for Students

Learning is a complex process that requires active participation from the learner. Asking questions is a big part of actively participating in learning. It helps the learner ensure they are on the right track and monitor and adjust their learning strategies.

This section describes several techniques you can teach students to help them ask better questions and find help when needed.

BE A GOOD LISTENER

The first step in asking good questions is to listen carefully to what's being said. See the section on listening on page 63 for strategies to help students develop their listening skills.

UNDERSTAND WHEN TO USE THE FOUR LEVELS OF QUESTIONS

To ask effective questions at the four levels, it is important that students know what kind of answer they are hoping to find. This can help them determine when to ask different kinds of questions. Knowing which question to ask and how to answer it assists in developing self-regulation for learning.

Share these guidelines:

- Factual questions are useful for clarifying basic information, such as vocabulary, important people, or facts that need to be recalled.
- Convergent questions help clarify understanding or interpretations of a lot of information, such as plot, themes, inference, and how things are done.
- Divergent questions are often creative. When asking or responding to them, students need to apply information from one source to another. For example, perhaps when learning about metamorphosis in science, students apply the concept of metamorphosis to another subject, such as metamorphosis in technology.
- Analytical questions require taking a position or making a claim and then defending it. As an example, students may be asked to identify the human factors involved in climate change and then defend why those are factors.

KNOW WHEN TO USE DEAD-END AND OPEN-ENDED QUESTIONS

Students need to know the purpose of dead-end and open-ended questions to use them effectively in learning. Share these guidelines and use the activity on page 83 to help students understand the difference.

- **Dead-end questions** have one right answer or can be answered with one word, such as *yes*, *no*, *true*, *false*, and so on. They are useful when students are seeking the efficiency of a quick answer or clarifying factual information. However, dead-end questions don't allow for any wiggle room, discussion, or difference in answers. Typically, these questions start with *who*, *what*, *when*, or *where*.
- **Open-ended questions** are those that require a great deal of information to suffice as an answer. Typically, these questions start with *how* or *why*. Thinking is required from both the questioner and the person answering the question. Open-ended questions build on information, make connections, and may even solicit additional considerations. They are useful when trying to deepen understanding or apply information from one subject to another.

QUESTION LIKE A SCHOLAR

Students answer questions, whereas scholars ask questions. To be successful in the future, students need to learn how to think and question like a scholar. According to Heacox and Cash (2020), "A scholar is one who learns and processes information with purpose and produces useful outcomes. A scholar also develops a scholarly disposition by being:

- open- and fair-minded
- inquisitive
- flexible in thinking and acting
- interested in seeking out reason
- immersed in acquiring more information
- respectful of and expecting diverse points of view" (Heacox and Cash 2020, 88)

KEEP A THINKING JOURNAL

Thinking can be a quick spurt of energy, or it can take a long time. One of the ways students can monitor their thinking is through using a Thinking Journal. A Thinking Journal can be either physical or virtual. It is a place for students to collect their thoughts, record their questions, and/or ponder answers. Thinking Journals can be divided into sections such as these:

- My thoughts/What I'm thinking
- Questions I ask myself
- Questions during class
- Answers to questions I'm asked
- Answers to questions during class

Students should have access to their Thinking Journals at all times of the day, because good thoughts and questions often come along at unexpected times. Writing or documenting thinking, including when they change their minds or adjust previous thoughts, is a habit of self-regulated learners. Try to build time into your schedule for students to write in their Thinking Journals to help them build this practice.

ASK FOR HELP

Some students may struggle in school because they don't know how to ask for help. Or they may be afraid to ask for help because they believe they may appear weak or "dumb." Reassure students that asking for help is actually a sign of intelligence, since everyone knows something, but no one knows everything. Turn asking for assistance from a peer into a chance for that person to shine. Share these ways students might ask for help:

- You seem to know this topic well. Can you please help me with . . .?
- I've hit a wall! I could use your support with . . .
- I thought I had a handle on this, but I'm struggling with . . .
- Your help with . . . is really appreciated.
- When you have a moment, would you look over . . . and offer me advice?

QUESTIONING GAMES

The use of games to teach thinking skills represents a dynamic and innovative approach to learning. By engaging learners in interactive and enjoyable experiences, games can foster critical thinking, problem-solving, and creativity. As educational paradigms continue to evolve, the integration of games will undoubtedly play a crucial role in unlocking the cognitive potential of learners. They're also fun!

TWENTY QUESTIONS

In this activity, students learn the difference between dead-end and open-ended questions.

Preparation: Select two pictures. They could be work of arts, pictures of a location, and so on. Don't select pictures that are too intricate, as students will be trying to re-create the pictures using questioning strategies. Do not show the pictures to students.

Process:

1. Pair up students. One student is Partner A, and the other student is Partner B. Partners sit back to back so they cannot see each other's materials.
2. Give each student one piece of paper for drawing. Give Partner A one of the pictures and Partner B the other picture. Tell students that they will ask questions about their partner's picture and use their partner's answers to try to re-create a drawing of the image.
3. Partner A draws first. They may ask only dead-end questions—those questions that can be answered using one word. After twenty questions have been asked, Partner A shares their drawing and Partner B shares the original picture. How close did Partner A come to re-creating the picture?
4. Now it's Partner B's turn to draw. However, Partner B may ask only open-ended questions about Partner A's image. (It is okay to use some dead-end questions to clarify.) After twenty questions have been asked, the students share and compare again. In general, Partner B's picture should be more detailed and closer to the original than Partner A's was.
5. After you've finished the activity, discuss as a group the importance of dead-end and open-ended questions and when to use them.

Other considerations: This activity can also be done as a class, where students ask you dead-end and open-ended questions to re-create an image or picture.

WHO/WHAT AM I?

Try this game when developing vocabulary, identifying parts of speech, learning about people who work in a specific field, exploring tools used in the kitchen/shop, and so on.

Preparation: Develop a list of terms for this game. Get a number of sticky notes equal to the number of students in your group. Write one term on each sticky note.

Process:

1. Place one sticky note on each student's back. Students do not see what is on their notes.
2. Play through two rounds of the game. Students pair up and ask and answer questions to determine what is written on the notes on their backs. You will need to assign or have students determine who is Partner A and who is Partner B.
   - Round 1: Partner A asks Partner B ten dead-end questions to find out what is on their note.
   - Round 2: Partner B asks Partner A ten dead-end and open-ended questions to find out what is on their note.
3. Discuss what students thought about the activity. Was it easier for one partner to determine what was written on their note?
4. Discuss the importance of using dead-end questions and open-ended questions. Also discuss the importance of content knowledge in asking and answering questions.

Study Methods That Work

Teachers often lament that students don't seem to know *how* to study. And students may think that studying is as simple as putting the information in front of them and committing it to memory. The act of learning is a complex and commonly misunderstood process, and knowing how to study is an important technique to master. Dr. Daniel Willingham (2023), renowned cognitive psychologist from Harvard University and professor of psychology at the University of Virginia, has summarized studying/learning through three principles:

1. Memory is the residue of thought.
2. Organization helps memory.
3. Probing memory improves memory.

Previous sections of this book have tackled some of the components of the first two principles. For example, note-taking helps students solidify information into memory, while staying organized helps them make connections between bits of information so they can quickly recall information from memory. This section focuses on the third principle: how to study to commit information to memory for future use.

Learning, like developing muscle strength, requires students to do things that may feel difficult and where they may not notice immediate success. Studying must go beyond preparing for tests and quizzes. It is most effective when it is a routine habit employed to commit information to memory and then use that information in multiple ways (see more on this in the section on home study on page 92).

When studying, it's important for students to consider the three dimensions of self-regulation: adjusting themselves to feel confident in learning (affect), using study methods known to increase memory and retention (behavior), and becoming self-efficacious learners (cognition).

This section shares several strategies for helping students build good study habits, as well as four effective study methods.

Strategies for Teachers

Teachers can make the act of studying a component of their instruction. When teaching a study habit or technique, be sure to demonstrate it first and have students copy you. As they continue to practice, they will refine the strategy to fit their needs.

Following are ways to help build students' habits of studying.

TEACH MNEMONICS

A mnemonic is a series of letters, words, or silly phrases that helps students remember information. You can think of mnemonics as memory tricks for recalling information (Willingham 2023). There are well-known mnemonics for every content area and many types of mnemonics. Do an internet search to find the best ones for your students. Here are a few examples to start with:

- **HOMES: Huron, Ontario, Michigan, Erie, Superior** (The Great Lakes of the United States)
- **PEMDAS: Parentheses, Exponents, Multiplication, Division, Addition, Subtraction** (order of operations)
- **Every Good Boy Does Fine: EGBDF** (order of musical notes on the lines of a staff in treble clef)
- **My Very Excellent Mother Just Served Us Nachos: Mercury, Venus, Earth, Mars, Jupiter, Saturn, Uranus, Neptune** (order of the planets in the solar system)

- **I** before **E** except after **C** (common order of these vowels when they appear next to each other in English words)
- The princi**pal** is your **pal** (tip for remembering how to spell the homophones *principal* and *principle)*

CREATE YOUR OWN STUDY GUIDES

Purchased materials, whether from an internet site or a publisher, may not be the best fit for your students and what you expect them to learn. It's better to create your own study guides. This way, students are sure to study what will be on your exam or measurement of achievement.

One of the best ways to help students study for an assessment is to prepare them for the structure of the questions that will be asked. When crafting study guides, be sure to include questions written in the same way that they will appear on the quiz or test. Making students aware of what they should study and what will be tested ensures that your assessments are fair and equitable. Even better than providing a teacher-created study guide is teaching students how to create their own study guides. See FPC Study Guides on page 87.

DEVELOP STUDY BUDDIES AND STUDY GROUPS

Study buddies and study groups encourage students to support each other in learning. Study buddies are long-term, prearranged partners who can assist each other in learning, studying at home, or completing tasks during or after class time. Study buddies can meet virtually or in person. The benefit of study buddies is that each student is ensured a partner in learning. Study buddies can be chosen by students or arranged by you based on similar or complementary personalities, needs, or other characteristics (Cash 2017).

Study groups are short-term, small groups that come together to study for an exam or a portion of content. You will want to keep these factors in mind when forming study groups:

- **The size of the group should be between three and six students.** This will ensure that each person has a part to play in the learning, and the group is more likely to stay focused.
- **Define where the groups will meet.** They can meet in person or virtually.
- **Schedule when the groups will meet.** It's best for the teacher to set a schedule to introduce students to the process and eventually allow the groups to decide when and how often they will meet.
- **Establish rules and roles for the group.** As with the schedule, you will want to set the rules and roles at first. After some practice, students should be able to set their own rules and decide their own roles. Keep in mind that rules for study groups should be positive in nature. Suggested rules include the following:
  - All students participate to the best of their abilities.
  - All students are encouraged to take intellectual risks without fear of reprisal.
  - All students are responsible to every member of the group.

  Roles can include the following:
  - **Captain.** This person is responsible for keeping the group on task and for setting the schedule and the agendas for each session.
  - **Timekeeper.** This person is responsible for ensuring that the group manages their time wisely and starts and ends on time.

- **Recorder.** This person is responsible for noting new ideas, drawing images, adding to other members' materials, and recording what was covered in each session.
- **Librarian:** This person is responsible for gathering materials the group may need for the next session.
- **Encourager:** This person is responsible for making sure everyone has the opportunity to share and participate to the best of their ability.
- **Reviewer:** This person is responsible for making sure everything has been documented correctly and that any presentation materials are accurate, aesthetically pleasing, viewable, and in the correct order.

Show students how to set a plan for their study group, how much should be reviewed in each session, and how to review materials. Using the FPC model (see below) may be a good beginning. Learning can be even more powerful when students work together to solidify content, develop responsibility, and collaborate!

Techniques and Tools for Students

A helpful way to reframe studying for students is to teach the concept of retrieval practice. Retrieval practice is what researchers call the process we go through to efficiently pull something from our memory—something that has been "learned." Practicing retrieving learned information from memory so that we can do it more quickly later is an effective way to study. Unfortunately, students aren't often taught this method, so it is much less common than practices such as reading over notes and rereading the textbook. But these are the *least* useful study strategies because they don't engage the brain in making connections or provide meaning to information (Willingham 2023).

Below are evidence-based retrieval-practice strategies you can teach students to improve their learning.

FPC STUDY GUIDES

A powerful study method for all students is to create their own study guides. The Factual/Procedural/Conceptual (FPC) Study Guide is a simple and effective model that students can use while reading text or observing videos, in class discussions, and during lessons. This method also gives students the opportunity to practice self-assessment, one of the most effective study habits.

In the FPC Study Guide model, there are three categories of information: low-level factual information (*who*, *what*, *where*, *when*), mid-level procedural information (*how*), and high-level conceptual information (*why*). To create a study guide, students write questions about the content at each of the levels and then then fill out the guide. Low-level questions provide foundational knowledge, mid-level questions expand on connections within the content, and high-level questions provide for reasoning and abstraction. See the next page for an example of a student's FPC Study Guide on the American Revolution.

Figure 10: **FPC Study Guide Example**

FACTUAL		PROCEDURAL		CONCEPTUAL	
Who, what, when, where questions	Answers	***How*** questions	Answers	***Why*** questions	Answers
What were the dates of the American Revolution?	April 19, 1775–September 3, 1783	How did the American Revolution begin?	It began with the Battles of Lexington and Concord in Massachusetts on April 19, 1775.	Why did the colonists feel compelled to revolt against British rule?	There were mounting feelings that there was increasing oppression by the British government, particularly through unfair taxation policies.
What document declared the American colonies' independence from Britain?	Declaration of Independence	How did the Declaration of Independence contribute to the American Revolution?	The DI was a formal declaration of the American colonies' separation from Britain, outlining their grievances against the British government and the desire to self-govern.		
When was the Treaty of Paris signed?	September 3, 1783	How did the Treaty of Paris come about?	Several factors contributed to the Treaty of Paris: • American victory at Yorktown • Lord North's resignation • American delegates travel to Paris • British recognition of U.S. independence • Western expansion in America		
Who were the patriots?	Colonists living in the British North American colonies who rebelled against the authority of the British crown	How did the American Revolution impact the world?	The AR inspired other revolutions around the world based on the ideas of democracy, individual rights, and republicanism.		
What was the largest battle during the war?	The Battle of Long Island, where 40,000 soldiers fought				

SQ4R

In 1948, Francis Robinson created this reading and review method to help students actively engage in reading text for greater understanding. It can be used throughout the learning process to help students solidify information into memory. Here's what it stands for and how to use it (Texas A&M University, n.d.):

- **Survey.** Students quickly skim the text for big ideas, headings, subheadings, figures, photos, and so on.
- **Question.** Based on what they surveyed, students write what they think may be in the materials and any initial questions they have.
- **Read.** Students read the text.
- **Recite.** In their own words, students recite key vocabulary or points that were highlighted in the text.
- **Review/Reflect.** After twenty-four hours, students go back over their notes and review what they learned from the reading.

Keys to using SQ4R:

- Students should try not to read every word when surveying the text.
- Students can turn headings and subheadings into questions to guide their reading and identify key concepts.
- While reading, students search for answers to the questions they wrote.
- Connecting new information to what students already know will make the information easier to remember.
- Students routinely return to their notes and questions to reinforce learning and ensure long-term retention.

THE POMODORO TECHNIQUE

This study method gets its name from the tomato-shaped kitchen timer that was used by its creator, Francesco Cirillo, as he tracked his work production. The method entails a series of timed, focused work intervals with breaks. Typically, the Pomodoro Technique uses twenty-five-minute intervals. I suggest starting students with shorter intervals. As they get older and/or more comfortable with the technique, they can increase the time of their intervals. Here's how it works (Glon 2021):

1. Students decide what needs to be done. They write it down in succinct terms.
2. Students set a timer for fifteen minutes.
3. Students work on the task they identified without interruption
4. When the timer goes off, students take a short break of no more than five minutes
5. Students repeat the process at least four times in a row.
6. At the end of the series, students can take a longer break and note how much work they completed.

Keys to using the Pomodoro Technique:

- Students should try to keep distractions to a minimum (avoid phones, social media, or other things that take their attention away from the task at hand).
- Students can track their progress by noting at the end of the cycle what they accomplished (How did the process feel? What did they do that worked or didn't work? How will they plan for next time?).
- Students can stop using timers as they get better at the process.

THE FEYNMAN TECHNIQUE

Developed by a world-renowned, Nobel Prize–winning theoretical physicist, Dr. Richard Feynman, this study method can help students learn complex concepts and ideas. Here's how it works (Farnam Street 2025):

1. Students first define the concept they are studying.
2. Next, students write out the information as if they are teaching it to a younger person or to someone who is unfamiliar with the topic. They may even want to draw pictures or create a simple story to help them teach it.
3. Students share what they created with someone else.
4. Then, they test their understanding of the information by asking the person questions to see if they understood what the student wrote. Students might ask things like:
    - What is the concept all about?
    - Where can you find it in the real world?
    - Was anything confusing? If so, what was it?
    - What questions do you have?

Keys to using the Feynman Technique:

- Students describe the information to someone else or pretend they are describing it to someone else—even doing it out loud.
- Students try to explain the information in the simplest terms possible.
- Students pay attention to where they are struggling in their explanation. This can indicate a lack of total understanding.
- Students can create an analogy for what they are trying to describe. For example, they might explain the concept of systems as a jigsaw puzzle—where smaller interconnected pieces, when put together correctly, create a whole picture.

Again, it's powerful for students to reflect on this method (How did the process feel? What did they do that worked or didn't work? How will they plan for next time?) after completing the four steps.

THE LEITNER SYSTEM

This system gets its name from German science journalist Sebastian Leitner. Here's how it works (Whelan 2019):

1. Students create flash cards of the information they want to study. Typically, the cards will have a term or concept on one side and the explanation on the other side.
2. Students make three containers to hold the flash cards. They label the containers:
    - Every Day
    - Every Other Day
    - Once a Week
3. All cards start in container 1 **(Every Day)**.
4. On the first day, students go through all the cards. If they are able to correctly define a card from container 1 **(Every Day)**, it goes into container 2 (**Every Other Day**). If not, it stays in container 1 (**Every Day)**.

5. The next day, students go through the remaining cards in container 1 (**Every Day**) again.
6. The third day, students begin the process again, starting with container 1 cards (**Every Day**) and moving on to container 2 cards (**Every Other Day**). If they answer container 2 cards correctly, they go into container 3 (**Once a Week**). If not, they stay in container 2 (**Every Other Day**).
7. Students continue in this way, reviewing the cards in each container as frequently as suggested.
8. Once all the cards have made it to container 3 (**Once a Week**), and students can correctly answer them, they have successfully mastered the material.

Keys to using the Leitner System:

- Students should try to be consistent and stay on track by reviewing the cards based on the box in which they are placed.
- When responding to the cards, students can try saying their answers out loud.
- Students can turn the system into a game with a study buddy, where one partner draws the card and the other responds.

TURNING AROUND QUESTIONS

A wonderful strategy, developed by Marian Small in her book *Good Questions: Great Ways to Differentiate Mathematics Instruction* (2012), is to teach students how to turn questions around. This method teaches students how to think deeply, differently, and creatively. It also reinforces having more than simple recall of information. To turn around questions, you can try these options:

- Pose the answer first.
- Replace words with numbers, letters, or blanks.
- Ask for complete sentences or require a number sentence.
- Change the question completely.

You might use these questions as a bell ringer activity as students enter the room, a sponge activity when you have a few minutes remaining in a class period and you don't want to begin a new topic, or on a quiz or test to check for understanding and creativity.

Examples:

Original question: What is half of 20?
Turn the question around: 10 is a fraction of a number. What could the fraction and number be?

Original question: What are Hamlet's fatal flaws?
Turn the question around: How do Hamlet's fatal flaws lead to appealing or appalling outcomes?

Original question: What is the chemical symbol for water?
Turn the question around: What transparent, odorless, inorganic compound and liquid is also known by the chemical symbol H_2O?

Home Study, Not Homework

Few issues in education cause more consternation than homework. The research on homework tends to be variable, depending on what is being studied. Conversations revolve around time spent on homework, amount of work completed during that time, and the advantages or disadvantages a student may encounter before, during, or after the work, to name a few.

Homework is often about compliance and the act of doing. When viewed this way, it has no real relationship to becoming a self-directed and lifelong learner. Studies routinely demonstrate that those who spend more time on homework do not necessarily outperform those who spend less time on it. In fact, some studies indicate that those who spend more time on homework "lag behind their peers in terms of achievement and achievement gains" (Trautwein 2007).

In my many years of teaching students and educators, I've found that there are two distinct foci of time devoted to actions outside the classroom: purpose and preparation. Purpose is related to "why" a student may interact with material after class time. Preparation corresponds to "readiness" for what's to come in the classroom in the near future. This is why the term "home study" is much more appropriate for what follows the school day.

Home study is about developing the skills and techniques of study, preparing oneself for the challenges ahead, developing a mindset of dedication, and being conscientious and motivated to be self-regulated. To be a lifelong learner, one must possess or develop the motivation and drive (affect) to take personal responsibility and control (behavior) of acquiring new knowledge and skills (cognition). Therefore, learning how to learn through the habits of home study can greatly benefit students in their approach toward success.

This section focuses on how to continue learning beyond the school day and shares various home-study strategies that will serve students well beyond the classroom.

Strategies for Teachers

As a teacher, you cannot force students to do the work you assign them as home study. You *can* use the following strategies to increase their motivation to get the work done. For strategies on helping students learn specific study methods, see the previous section (page 85).

SHARE THE PURPOSE OF HOME-STUDY WORK

Often, students do not understand the purpose of assigned home-study work. Try to be crystal clear with students about the purpose of the work you're assigning.

- **Practice (skill development).** Practice is an essential component of developing mastery. Home-study work for practice must be monitored and checked for accuracy. Effective practice is targeted at content where students have limitations or weaknesses in skill development. This means that students should not be wasting time practicing something they already know or can do just because. This also means that students need a way to quickly check their work to ensure that their practice is effective.
- **Preview/preparation (building background knowledge).** To increase the pace in the classroom, you may assign a prereading or a review of materials so as to not use class time for gathering lower levels of information. This can be done by reading ahead in the textbook, prereading a difficult chapter that will be reviewed and discussed in the next class period, or reading articles or reviewing websites to introduce, reinforce, or review a topic.
- **Completing tasks that were assigned during class time (developing time-management skills).** If there isn't enough time during the class period or students chose to use class time unwisely, home study can be used to complete materials needed for the next class period.

Avoid using home-study work as a punishment, especially if you didn't leave students enough time to complete an assignment. If a student didn't use class time wisely, try to find out why they were unable to complete the work. This is important, because if the student didn't understand the material or didn't have the skills to do what was required, sending it home won't ensure they do the work correctly.

- **Project development (problem-finding/solving skills).** Often, learning in the classroom culminates in a larger product. The best way to find out if students fully understand what they are learning is through having them find a problem, solve the problem, and submit the solution to an authentic audience. This may be one of the purposes of home study. Projects typically require several due dates and a number of steps. In addition to practicing problem-finding and problem-solving skills, project development can include planning, organization, time management, setting priorities, and applying learned information. Be clear about the purposes behind the project so students are completely aware of what they should do and what they are learning.
- **Developing responsibility.** In the early years, home study may be used to develop student responsibility and independence. A teacher can assign students a task, such as reading a book to a caregiver and then reporting on how the read went. If the purpose of the home study is to develop responsibility, be sure that the task does not impact a final grade and that it is not for the purpose of practice. You may give the action a nonnumerical notation, such as + (meaning completed), – (meaning uncompleted), or *I* (meaning incomplete).
- **Test/assessment preparation.** Home study can be used as a time to prepare for quizzes, tests, or other assessments. One of the best ways to prepare students for an assessment is to have them create questions that might be on the assessment. See the section on inquiry (page 78) for ways to teach students to develop good questions.
- **Connecting learning to real life (authentic applications).** Students are more motivated whey they see the relevance of their studies to real-life situations or experiences. Making connections and applying in-class learning to solve authentic problems outside of the classroom can enhance engagement.

Techniques and Tools for Students

Some of the most important skills for students to develop during the school years are those for studying and completing assignments at home. To be well prepared for a lifetime of learning, students must possess strategies for studying and completing work outside of the classroom. Those students who attend but don't successfully complete post-secondary school often lack effective study habits, making it difficult for them to get coursework done outside of the classroom (Strauss 2016). Studying is a process with specific requirements to ensure that time is used efficiently, resources are used effectively, and supports are available when needed.

When teaching home-study strategies, be sure to introduce them either one-by-one or in small doses, depending on the age of students and their abilities to manage themselves outside the classroom. Consider making each strategy a separate lesson that students practice until it becomes a habit.

SET A REGULAR STUDY TIME

To get the most out of their time after school, students can set a specific minimum amount of time (see the ten-minute rule on page 137) to study and identify a consistent time of day for study. Even if students are not assigned homework, they can use their set study time to read a book, magazine, or newspaper or to investigate websites related to what they are learning in school. Review strategies for time management on page 51 as well as the lesson about chronotypes with students to help them determine the best time for them to study.

CREATE A DISTRACTION-FREE STUDY SPACE

Students might study at the kitchen table, in their bedroom, or in a quiet corner in a shared living space. In some cases, students may need to look to the public or school library or a community room within their building complex. Wherever they find a learning space, students should ensure that the space has good lighting, that they have access to all materials they may need (include the internet), and that they have pleasant surroundings so as not to be distracted. Share the checklist on page 127 to help students set up their space for success, and review the section on obstacles (page 55) for strategies to help students overcome those challenges to home study that they can plan for.

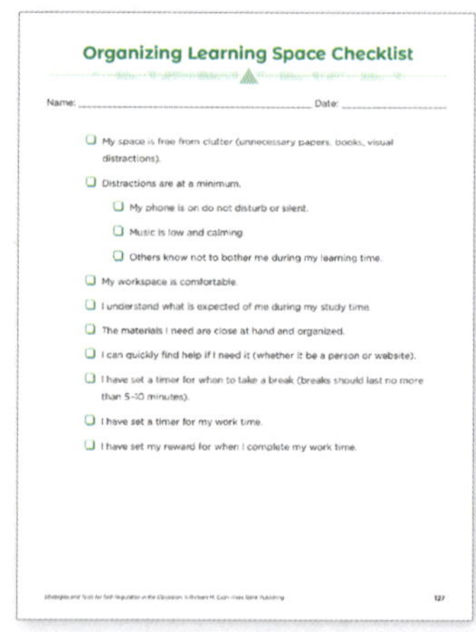

Organizing Learning Space Checklist

Name: ______________________ Date: ____________

- ❑ My space is free from clutter (unnecessary papers, books, visual distractions).
- ❑ Distractions are at a minimum.
  - ❑ My phone is on do not disturb or silent.
  - ❑ Music is low and calming.
  - ❑ Others know not to bother me during my learning time.
- ❑ My workspace is comfortable.
- ❑ I understand what is expected of me during my study time.
- ❑ The materials I need are close at hand and organized.
- ❑ I can quickly find help if I need it (whether it be a person or website).
- ❑ I have set a timer for when to take a break (breaks should last no more than 5–10 minutes).
- ❑ I have set a timer for my work time.
- ❑ I have set my reward for when I complete my work time.

127

MANAGE STUDY TIME

Encourage students to parcel out how much time they will spend on each subject or class's homework during their set amount of study time. Advise them to work on the hardest materials first and easier materials last and to not spend too much time on any one piece of work. As an example, for a sixty-minute study period, a student may parcel their time like so:

- twenty minutes devoted to math
- five-minute break
- twenty minutes devoted to working on an essay
- five-minute break
- ten minutes devoted to reading

Review the section on time management (page 51) for more ideas for helping students manage study time.

GET ORGANIZED

Being organized can greatly increase the efficiency and effectiveness of students' home study. File folders, boxes, computer files, and jump drives are all appropriate methods for organizing materials. Students may need someone to help them set up a system and they may need to try a few systems before they land on the one that works best for them. Review the section on organization (page 31) for more ideas.

IDENTIFY LEARNING PREFERENCES

When students know their learning preferences, they can apply those preferences to their home study. While the jury is still out on how effective learning types are in the classroom, some researchers have shown some positive effects of using preferred ways of learning (or learning styles) during study periods (Ogut, Senol, and Yildirim 2017). See the section in part I (page 21) for strategies to help students identify their learning preferences.

TAKE BREAKS

During study time, students should aim to take a two- to five-minute break around every twenty minutes. The human brain can only pay attention to one thing for short periods of time without needing to adjust or redirect itself to avoid cognitive fatigue. Cognitive fatigue strains the brain's mental performance and can lead to disorganization, lack of focus, and mistakes. During study breaks, students can stretch, take a walk, or get a glass of water.

AVOID GETTING STUCK BEFORE GETTING STARTED

Procrastination, or the inability to get started, can have a dramatic effect on students' study and achievement. Everyone suffers from various degrees of procrastination, from minor ("I'll do that later") to major ("I will do anything *except* that"). Minor procrastination usually just prolongs the situation, whereas major procrastination may end in disaster.

If students are getting stuck at getting started, encourage them to think about why they may be avoiding the work and ways to get themselves inspired, motivated, or moving. It can also be helpful for students to do a self-regulation self-check and adjust their affect, behavior, and cognition. To do so, they can ask, answer, and act upon the following questions:

- Affect: What am I feeling right now? Why am I feeling this way? What can I do to feel better about what needs to be done?
- Behavior: What am I doing now? What should I be doing now? What will I do to get the work completed?
- Cognition: What thoughts are going through my mind now? How can I adjust the way I am thinking about the work that needs to be done? What thinking tools will I need to apply during the work ahead?

PLAN FOR HOW TO FIND HELP

Everyone needs help sometimes. Knowing whom to ask, how to ask, and when to ask for help is a strength, not a deficit. Students can create a plan for where they can go for help when they get stuck completing work at home. (See also the section on overcoming obstacles (page 55) for more on asking for help.)

SELF-ASSESS

Self-assessment is one of the most beneficial study strategies. It helps students monitor their learning and adjust when there is a lack of understanding, increases self-directed learning, and promotes academic integrity. To self-assess, students can write five questions about the materials they covered (no need to answer them, as a well-worded question can tell a lot about how much a person knows or understands about a topic) or answer any chapter-end questions in their textbook to check their understanding. Routine self-assessment can have a powerful effect on student achievement.

REFLECT ON STUDY

Like self-assessment, reflection can have a positive effect on learning. Reflection time doesn't need to be extensive. In fact, devoting two to five minutes to it at the end of every study period can be enough. Students can ask themselves questions about what they were studying, call a friend to discuss their learning or the material, or talk to a parent or guardian about what they just studied. They can also ask themselves the following questions about their affect, behavior, and cognition:

- Affect: How do I feel now that the study time is over? What motivated/didn't motivate me during my study time? How can I ensure I feel good about studying next time?
- Behavior: What distracted me during study time? How did I manage my time/stay organized? What will I do better next time?
- Cognition: How did today's study time help me become a better learner? What thinking tools did I practice during my study time? What tools will I use next time?

PHONE A FRIEND

The concept of phoning a friend for help doesn't need to be exclusive to game shows! It can be an effective strategy for students to use when they get stuck during their home study too. Guide students in practicing this strategy with partners during class time to grow their comfort in asking peers for help during home study.

Process:

1. Have each student select a study buddy or friend, or arrange students into partnerships.
2. For each pair, designate one student to be the quiz show contestant and the other the friend that the contestant will phone.
3. Throughout the week, the contestant must contact the friend to ask for help getting organized, assistance in staying focused, or encouragement to keep going. After one week, the roles are reversed.
4. After students have practiced the routine of being the contestant and the friend, the partnership should have become natural and supportive, one that students can continue to lean on in the future.

Technology

As of this book's writing, there's not yet a lot of research on the use of technology in the classroom and for study purposes since the learning landscape changed due to the Covid-19 pandemic. And with the onset of artificial intelligence (AI) and the super advancements in tech, it's difficult to know what's coming next in learning technologies. Increasing the benefits of tech for learning and reducing its challenges should be the focus of using technology in study and in the classroom.

Technology can be used for myriad purposes in learning, such as researching topics, building websites, checking assignments, communicating with teachers and peers, and so on. And technology can enhance or damage self-regulation for learning. Screen time can have an immense impact on what students pay attention to (affect), whether they invest in face-to-face interaction (behavior), and how they think about themselves and their positions in the world (cognition). Learning to balance interactions with technology and various media platforms can increase students' connections to others and the world around them.

This section looks at technology more broadly and how it can enhance learning, motivate students, and be a tool for study.

Strategies for Teachers

When teaching students to use technology to improve their learning, modeling a balanced use of tech is a great place to start. Technology can easily overwhelm students' lives with a constant flow of, and instant access to, information. Teaching students how to balance tech use can help them lead happier lives and have greater well-being.

Here are a few more tips and tools for using tech in your classroom, based on writing by Jamie K. for the nonprofit organization Common Sense (2023).

DEBRIEF OFTEN

When using technology in the classroom, set a timer for ten minutes. After the ten minutes are up, have students engage in tech-free activities:

- having a conversation about the content
- discussing the benefits and challenges of the technology
- doing a physical activity, such as getting up and stretching
- having a snack or a drink of water
- doing a few deep breathing exercises

SET CLEAR GUIDELINES

Set clear and easy-to-understand guidelines for when and how to use technology in the classroom. Stay true to the guidelines and know that students will need constant reminders.

CREATE A CLASSROOM POLICY FOR TECH USE

Your policy should be in line with any schoolwide policies. Share the policy with students and their families and have students and caregivers sign it to agree to the commitment. This is especially important when using school-provided technology and networks.

SHARE THE PURPOSE OF TECH USE

Sharing the purpose behind why students are using tech in class promotes active versus passive consumption. When students know the reason for the tech, they are more likely to respect the media as a learning tool rather than a toy. Consider purposes like these:

- extending beyond the text in the classroom
- discovering different viewpoints
- observing short media clips
- sharing new knowledge
- studying a topic of interest
- writing and editing a document
- communicating via email or other media
- posting to a group chat or message board
- computing
- connecting to a learning activity associated with classroom discussions
- creating spreadsheets, charts, graphics, or other visual documents
- creating presentations

CREATE A FLEXIBLE LEARNING ENVIRONMENT

Your classroom can include areas where students can use technology together or alone. Providing a flexible learning space may be a challenge in some settings. If your space is limited, consider removing furniture or storage units that you don't routinely use. This may require some planning or setup ahead of time to make sure that materials are readily available. The idea is to make the learning space as pliable as possible, so that it is suitable for whatever needs to be done.

ACCEPT THAT AI IS HERE TO STAY

Rather than avoiding AI, try to integrate it into lessons and daily routines. What's most important is to teach students ethical ways to use AI in their assignment construction and to avoid the temptation to have AI do their work for them. The number one way to encourage students to ethically use AI is to model it for them. Every time you use images, ideas, or text from an internet source, cite it! Even if the materials seem to be from an "open source," it's still a good idea to cite where you gathered your materials.

Techniques and Tools for Students

Mobile devices and technology are an integral part of students' lives. The job of educators is not to dissuade the use of the devices and technology, but to teach students how to use them appropriately and during the right times. Here are a few ways you can help students use technology for learning.

PRACTICE DIGITAL SAFETY

Part of using tech for learning is using tech wisely. Share these ten tips for digital safety with students. There are also numerous websites that have more information you can consult for how to keep students safe online.

1. **Keep device surfaces clean.** This can significantly reduce the risk of transmission of viruses and other communicable germs.
2. **Keep software up to date.** This reduces the risk of digital viruses, ransomware, and malware.

3. **Create unique passwords.** Strong passwords are usually at least twelve characters long and include letters, numbers, and special characters (# $ % &). To remember passwords, students can download a password manager that will produce unique passwords for each account. Advise them to avoid using phrases, song lyrics, names of pets or family members, birthdates or years, or other recognizable words. A good password may be a statement students say privately to themselves often (such as "IEnjoyPlayPiano4MyLoved1's).
4. **Use multi-factor authentication.** This authentication process will often use facial recognition or a code sent in an email or text as a security measure in addition to a password.
5. **Think before you click.** Tell students not to open files on their devices from people they do not know or files from people they do know when they weren't expecting to receive something from them. Opening unknown files can lead to malicious attacks on devices, release students' sensitive information, and even destroy their devices.
6. **Don't open suspicious links.** Phishing is a common practice by fraudulent individuals or companies to get a person to reveal personal information. The emails may look "real" but will often come from an odd email address. Again, if students didn't seek out the information, they should think before they click. They can also report the phishing to their email provider, internet service provider, and/or the social media platform.
7. **Use secure connections.** Many public wireless networks and hotspots are unsecured, meaning others can potentially see students' information and what they are doing as they are using the Wi-Fi. If students must use an unsecured network, they should avoid putting in passwords or other sensitive information.
8. **Back up work.** Many programs now have an automatic save, but not always. It's always a good idea to save work to an external drive (such as a jump drive) as well as to a "cloud" service. This will ensure that students' hard work doesn't get lost in the case of a power failure or device malfunction.
9. **Check settings.** Teach students that each time they download an application or game or get a new device, it is a good idea to look through the settings. There are ways to regulate when they get notifications, set privacy and security options, and control whether a game or download can run in the background when they're not actively using it. Deleting applications, games, and other platforms that they no longer need or don't use can help their devices run more quickly and safely.
10. **Share with care.** This is especially true on social media platforms. Students should not share personal information about themselves, their family, or their friends. Some nefarious individuals may be able to hack the information or use personal situations to bully, be malicious, or jeopardize future endeavors. Students can learn to think about how the information they post online might be used for or against them.

USE AI AS A STUDY TOOL

AI can be an exceptional tool to help students prepare for quizzes, exams, and major tests. Students can use it to create preparatory quizzes or tests, make flash cards, outline study guides, and create other study supports.

Model for students how to choose a favorite platform and then load in the information. AI will do all the work of creating study support materials, exam-style readings, and assignment prompts. The platform can even be prompted to differentiate for individual students' needs and abilities. AI can grade practice assessments, so students have immediate feedback on their preparation for an exam.

Be sure to have your students check the information for accuracy, or review what the students have created with AI to ensure that it is valuable.

USING GENERATIVE AI TO PROMOTE STUDENT-DRIVEN INQUIRY

AI has the potential to transform education, research, and many other fields. By harnessing the power of natural language processing and machine learning algorithms, generative AI can create questions that promote deeper understanding, critical thinking, and personalized learning experiences. However, it is important to address the challenges and ethical considerations associated with AI and ensure that human oversight remains a key component of the process. With careful implementation and ongoing refinement, AI can be a valuable tool in students' quests for knowledge and discovery.

Process:

1. Guide students to access an open AI resource or a closed AI platform that features a questioning app.
2. Provide students with the following prompt: "What good questions could I ask and address that would develop or deepen my understanding of . . .?"
3. Instruct students to complete the prompt with one of the following:
    - the standard being addressed and assessed
    - the subject or skill being studied
    - the text, topic, or technique being taught
4. After the questions have been generated by AI, encourage students to extend their learning. They might try the following activities offline:
    - Discuss the questions generated by the AI and brainstorm how to enhance or extend the questions.
    - Use the questions to engage in an inquiry-based learning experience.
    - Create a set of class questions they can use to strengthen, support, or stretch their learning.

Based on the work of Erik Francis, author of *Deconstructing Depth of Knowledge* and *Inquiring Minds Want to Learn*. Used with permission.

PART IV:
Reviewing and Reflecting on Learning

The fourth phase in the learning process is to review and reflect on what was learned. This phase tends to be overlooked, but it is a critical component of learning that can set up a positive beginning to a new learning cycle. The review and reflection phase must be a consistent part of instruction and of the classroom environment.

Teaching students how to review and reflect is also a vital component of a holistic education. These practices promote emotional intelligence, reduce stress and anxiety, improve academic performance, and foster personal growth and resilience. By incorporating the following review and reflection strategies into instruction, you can create a supportive and nurturing learning environment that empowers students to thrive academically, emotionally, and personally. In doing so, you equip students with the skills and mindset necessary to navigate the complexities of life and achieve their full potential.

So many students are overscheduled, stressed out, and anxious about the world around them. When they do have downtime, they may not know how to truly unwind emotionally, physically, and mentally. Therefore, this phase of learning also includes strategies to encourage students to reward themselves, relax, and recharge for the next learning challenge.

Self-Assessment

An important part of developing self-regulation for learning is to be able to assess and reflect on the *what*, *how*, and *why* of learning. This is an interaction between the teacher and the learner. The teacher uses students' self-assessments to ensure that students know what they are to learn, observe how well students are able to do or show what they learned, and ensure that students understand why the information was worth learning. For students, self-assessment is a form of reflection that can solidify the acquisition of factual information (*what*), procedural knowledge (*how*), and conceptual understandings (*why*).

Self-assessment is different from self-evaluation. Self-evaluation is when the student grades their own work against a set criteria, such as a rubric or standard, often devised or imposed by the teacher. Self-assessment is a continuous process that starts before the work begins and continues while work is in progress and when revising work prior to publication. "The primary purpose of engaging students in careful self-assessment is to boost learning and achievement" (Andrade 2010, 3).

Self-regulated learners are the definitive sources of their own learning. By embracing the principles of confidence, goal setting, monitoring learning, perseverance, and reflection, they unlock their potential for academic success and lifelong growth. They are directly involved in how they are feeling about what they are learning (affect), what they are doing that is working or not working (behavior), and the thinking tools they are developing to further their knowledge (cognition). This section focuses on helping students self-assess their learning by walking you through the process of developing a learning log.

Strategies for Teachers

A learning log is an educational tool used to promote reflection and self assessment. It is a personal record where students document their learning experiences, reflections, and progress over time. This practice is widely used in various educational settings, from primary schools to higher education institutions, and it is valued for its ability to foster self-awareness and critical thinking.

The components of a learning log include, but are not limited to, the following:

- date
- learning activities
- reflections (what I did, how I felt)
- feedback received from teachers or peers and the student's response to the feedback
- goals based on reflections and feedback

There are numerous types of learning logs available. Page 152 shares a log students can use or adapt to their needs. You can also do an internet search for learning logs to find one you and your students feel most comfortable using. The strategies that follow include ideas for helping students create and keep learning logs.

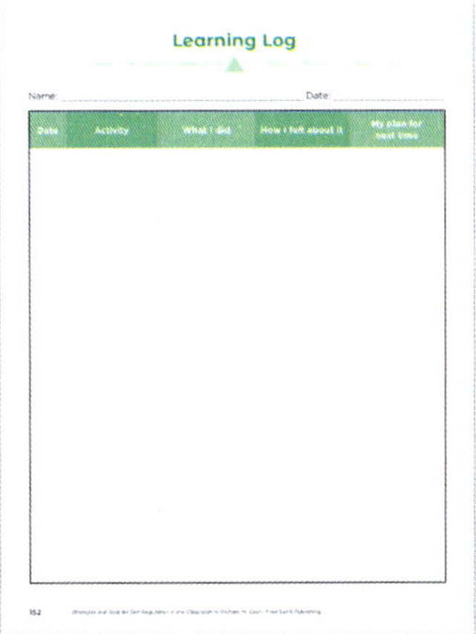
Learning Log

Name: Date:

Date	Activity	What I did	How I felt about it	My plan for next time

SHARE THE GOALS OF LESSONS AND ACTIVITIES

Clearly articulate the objectives, standards, and/or outcomes of classroom lessons and activities. Be sure to frame them in a way so that students completely understand what is expected of them. They will need to write the objectives, standards, and/or outcomes in their own words in their learning logs.

COCREATE RUBRICS

Creating rubrics with students encourages a deeper understanding of what you expect of them, increases students' ownership of their work, and gives them a voice in how they are assessed, leading to better self-regulated learners. The cocreated rubric should be included as the first page of the learning log.

Follow these steps to cocreate a rubric:

1. Put students into small groups. Provide each group with two examples of a final product for the activity or lesson. One example is a high-quality product, while the other is lower in quality.
2. Have students examine the examples, marking them with a green highlighter where the example is strong and a yellow highlighter where the example is weak. There is no marking for areas in the middle.
3. Using the "snowballing" technique to review the examples:
   - Small groups partner up and note where there was agreement on the strong and weak examples. Groups continue to double in size until everyone is in a large group.
   - At each step of snowballing, groups should come to an agreement on what qualities make an example strong or weak.
4. Once the groups have come together as a class, on a T-chart, document the strong and weak qualities of the examples (see sample chart below).

Figure 11: T-Chart Example

STRONG WORK	WEAK WORK
elaborate language	boring language
everything spelled correctly	lots of spelling errors
neat work	sloppy work
interesting	dull

5. As a class, discuss how to transform the weak qualities into strong qualities.
6. Review the strong qualities and categorize them into criteria for a rubric. For an essay, criteria might include the following: punctuation, grammar, form, style, aesthetics, original ideas, supported with evidence, and organization.
7. With students, narrow down the list to the five most important criteria for the product.

8. Define, with students' help, the rating scale for the rubric. For example, if "supported with evidence" is included on the rubric, the scale may go something like this:

    1 = little to no evidence

    2 = some evidence or unequally applied

    3 = good quality evidence or well applied

    4 = exceptional-quality evidence

HAVE STUDENTS MARK UP THEIR WORK

This is a self-assessment process. Using different colored pencils or pens, students underline in one color where they feel they are doing well, in another color where they are not sure if their work is accurate, and in a third color where they feel they are not doing well. Have students use this strategy on homework, quizzes, work samples, lab reports, and so on. Students' self-marked work is then shared with peers or the teacher for review.

PROVIDE TIME TO REVISE

Give students ample opportunity and time to make corrections, improvements, and revisions prior to turning in their work. This is not the publication point; it is the time for students to make any final adjustments before their assignments are handed in.

SHARE YOUR LEARNING JOURNEY

Learning something new is a challenge for everyone. The process one goes through when dealing with learning challenges, failures, and successes can greatly impact feelings of self-worth. So share your learning journey with students, being sure to talk about your assessment of your learning. Whether you're completing a graduate class to further your career or learning to play the violin for fun, your students will enjoy hearing about you as a learner.

Techniques and Tools for Students

This section is devoted to helping students set up learning logs where they monitor, assess, and reflect on their learning. By creating learning logs, students can follow their progress from beginning to end. A learning log may also double as a portfolio assessment.

BEFORE WORK BEGINS

To effectively self-assess their learning, students need to have complete knowledge of the factual, procedural, and conceptual goals of the lesson or activity before their work begins. In this section of the learning log, students show what they already know about the topic, share what they are interested in learning about it, and show that they understand the *what*, *why*, and *how* of the learning. Following are a few ways to help students complete this section of their learning logs:

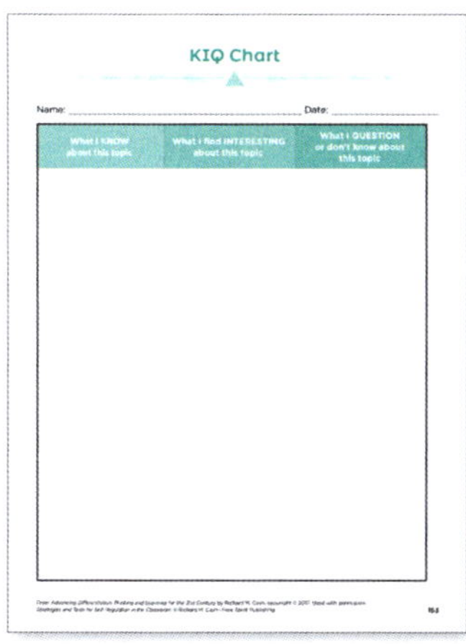
KIQ Chart

Name: Date:

What I KNOW about this topic	What I find INTERESTING about this topic	What I QUESTION or don't know about this topic

- **Have students write, in their own words, the expectations of the lesson or activity.**
- **Cocreate a rubric with students** (see above) with notations that describe and define each of the criteria and the value to each level within the rubric.

› **Have students complete KIQ Charts (page 153).** Depending on students' ages, you could also have them complete the I Chart (page 154) or the What Interests Me: Topic Preview form (page 155) as other tools to uncover background knowledge and build interest in the topic.

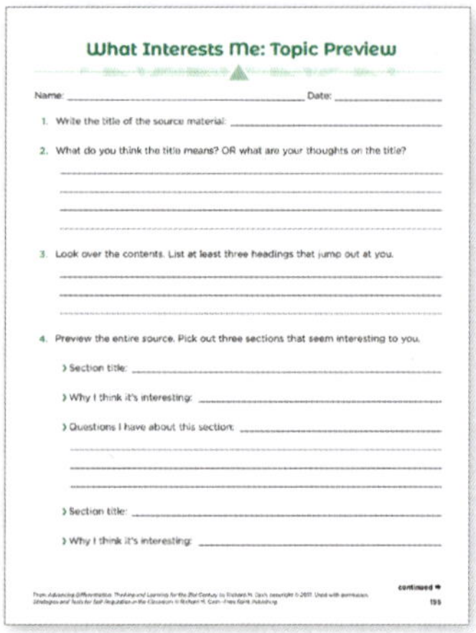
What Interests Me: Topic Preview

Name: Date:

1. Write the title of the source material:
2. What do you think the title means? OR what are your thoughts on the title?
3. Look over the contents. List at least three headings that jump out at you.
4. Preview the entire source. Pick out three sections that seem interesting to you.

› Section title:
› Why I think it's interesting:
› Questions I have about this section:
› Section title:
› Why I think it's interesting:

WHILE THE WORK IS IN PROGRESS

Another part of self-assessment is monitoring and adjusting work in progress. Allowing students opportunities to review their work before it is turned in or published can reduce stress and eliminate perfectionistic behaviors. In this portion of the learning log, students document what they are learning, how they are doing with developing skills, and why they are learning what they are learning. Here's what this section includes:

› rough drafts, work samples, lab reports, quizzes, or other examples that show students' progress

› completed and graded homework

› checklists or to-do lists

› notes from teacher-to-student or student-to-student conferencing

› progress monitoring on the cocreated rubric

› daily reflections on learning (see the Personal Reflection form on page 157 for a format and prompts students can use)

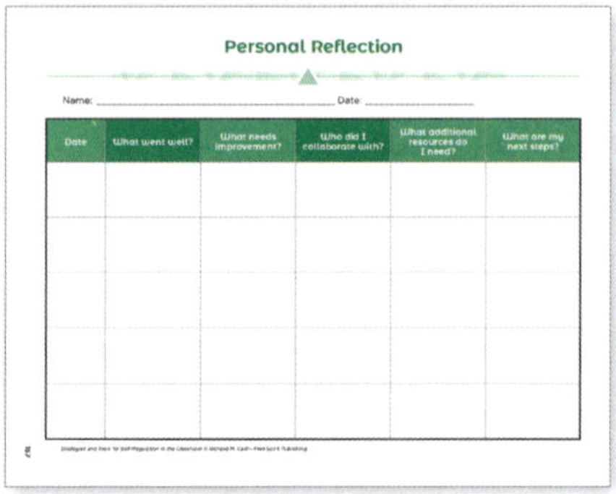
Personal Reflection

Name: Date:

Date	What went well?	What needs improvement?	Who did I collaborate with?	What additional resources do I need?	What are my next steps?

PRIOR TO PUBLICATION

Students should document revisions and improvements they make prior to the publication of their work. In this case, "publication" is considered the time when work is sent in for expert or final examination. Expert examinations are usually done by an outside discipline professional (such as a historian reviewing students' historical research or a working artist reviewing students' artwork), while final examinations are often done by the classroom teacher. Here's what this section of the learning log includes:

› a review of the cocreated rubric, noting where corrections, improvements, and revisions were made

› marked corrections, improvements, and revisions made based on in-progress assessments or peer reviews

› additional drafts, work samples, lab reports, quizzes, or other examples that show progress

› completed checklists or to-do lists

› records of teacher-to-student or student-to-student conferencing

CHECK YOUR UNDERSTANDING

This activity can be used in any content area to help students self-assess their understanding of the written word.

Process:

1. Give each student a Check Your Understanding handout (page 158).
2. Instruct students to read the statement at the top of the page. Explain that they will have one minute to draw a picture that illustrates the statement. They should use their imaginations and include as much detail as they can in their drawings.
3. After the minute is up, invite students to review their illustrations:
   - How well does their illustration show their understanding of the statement?
   - What could they add to make their illustration more understandable?
   - How might someone else interpret their illustration?
4. After students have reviewed their illustrations, have them share their drawings with partners, asking these questions:
   - How well does my illustration show my understanding of the statement?
   - What could I add to make my illustration more understandable?
   - What is your interpretation of my illustration?

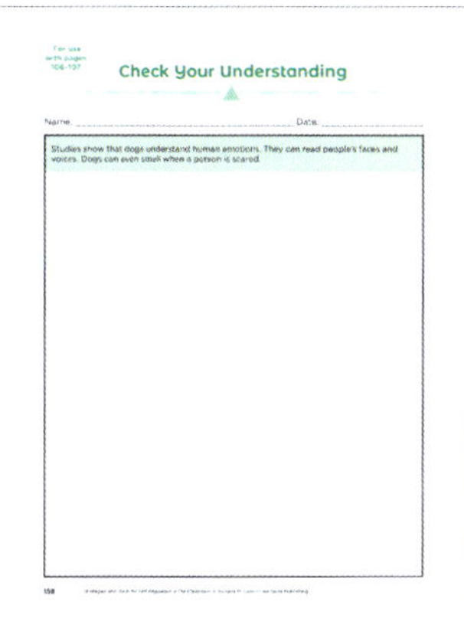
For use with pages 106–107

Check Your Understanding

Name: ______ Date: ______

Studies show that dogs understand human emotions. They can read people's faces and voices. Dogs can even smell when a person is scared.

Reflection

Reflection is the thinking process a person goes through to evaluate an experience or activity. It has a profound effect on one's growth as a learner, personal accomplishments, and sense of relevance and meaning making. Reflection transforms concrete experiences into abstract concepts (Chang 2019).

Reflection is a critical component in developing the cognitive dimension of self-regulation for learning. It engages the learner in analyzing their learning process, identifying areas where improvement is needed, and refining their strategies when necessary. Self-regulated learners take ownership of their learning by actively reflecting on their motivation (affect), on what they are doing that is working and not working (behavior), and how they might better plan for next time (cognition). Based on the work by Costa and Kallick (2008), reflection should accomplish three things:

- promote students' awareness of their own learning
- assist students in taking responsibility for their own learning
- define students' own growth in learning

But for reflection to be a useful tool in learning, students must be taught *how* to reflect. Most of the time, students are not taught, nor are they asked, to reflect on their learning. And when they do reflect on learning, they often respond with shallow statements, such as "I liked this lesson," "I didn't think the activity was worth my time," or "This assignment was easy." While these statements may share how student felt about a lesson, activity, or assignment, they aren't true reflections on the learning that happened. This section shares strategies to help students better reflect on their learning experience so they can become more self-aware and adaptable and make continuous improvements toward academic success.

Strategies for Teachers

Because reflection is an essential part of the learning process, it is an important component of the instructional process. Below are considerations for making reflection an integral part of learning. Keep in mind that students' learning logs (see the section on self-assessment on page 103) can provide tangible evidence they can use to reflect on their growth, both academically and in their ability to self-regulate for learning.

REFLECT ON YOUR INSTRUCTION

As with most things, modeling how you reflect is one of the best ways to show students how to do it. You can do this at the end of a lesson using statements about your affect, behavior, and cognition in instruction. This is also a helpful strategy for your professional development.

- Affect: "I felt this lesson went well. I was happy to see how engaged you were during the lesson."
- Behavior: "I worked hard to ensure that my lesson had proper flow and was sequenced for you to follow."
- Cognition: "My plan for next time is to be well prepared, so you can continue to be successful."

TEACH VARIOUS REFLECTION METHODS

Before asking students to independently reflect on their learning, it is important to teach (and model) various strategies for reflecting. See the techniques and tools for students for a selection of methods.

MAKE REFLECTION A HABIT

Reflection should be a common practice, not a special event. Make it routine by planning reflection time into your lessons and activities. You only need a few minutes each day or period. At first, it's likely that reflection will feel forced, but the more students do it, the more they will make this time their own and the more they will come to see its value.

To start, encourage students to reflect before, during, and after learning. For example, at the beginning of a lesson, ask students to think about what they already know about the topic and what they are interested in learning about it. During the lesson, pause and invite students to reflect on the lesson objectives and how they are being addressed. Finally, at the end the end of the lesson, have each students create an exit ticket with the following items:

- what they learned
- how the lesson objectives were applied
- what they anticipate will come next
- how this learning is connected to other subjects
- what they may do with the content in the future

When providing time for students to reflect on their learning, be sure to offer various ways they can reflect. Some students enjoy writing about their learning, while others may prefer to reflect by talking with you or with a partner.

USE THE ABCS OF SELF-REGULATION IN REFLECTION

Try to ensure that students are connecting their affect, behavior, and cognition to the reflection process.

- Affect: What were your feelings heading into this activity/lesson? How did those feelings drive your attention?
- Behavior: Were you sure about what to do throughout this activity/lesson? In what ways did you/can you seek out the help you might need?
- Cognition: As you plan for upcoming activities/lessons, what goals or plans will you set for yourself to be successful?

ENCOURAGE DEEPER REFLECTION

As students learn the skill of reflecting on learning, they may need prompting to take their reflections deeper. Try these prompts:

- Tell me more.
- Help me understand your thinking.
- Where did you find your information?
- What is the evidence you have that supports your thinking?
- Who can add to this information?

USE CONFERENCING TO ENCOURAGE REFLECTION

Teacher-to-student conferencing can be done with individual students or in small groups. In these conferences, ask open-ended questions that prompt students to think deeply about where they are in their learning and where they are going. Use questions like these:

- Of all the elements in your project, which ones are you most proud of and why?

- How might you improve on your project or learning?
- Whom do you rely upon when things get difficult?
- What are the most difficult or challenging factors of this project?
- If you were to start over, what would you change and how would you change it?

Peer-to-peer conferencing builds relationships and fosters collaboration and knowledge sharing. Most importantly, peer-to-peer conferences create an environment where learning is a community event and where all learners support each other in learning. Following are a few guidelines for peer-to-peer conferencing:

- Be an active and empathic listener.
- Offer constructive feedback that is positive and specific.
- Be respectful.
- Be supportive of each other's growth.
- Remember, learning is a community event, not an isolated race.

Techniques and Tools for Students

Reflecting on learning can be done individually or with a group. When reflecting individually, the goal of reflection is to find personal relevance to and meaningfulness in the learning activity. When reflecting with a group, the goal is to enhance the learning experience through hearing others' insights and ideas.

Teach students the following strategies for reflecting on learning. During reflection time, they can choose which method to use. Additional reflection strategies can be found in chapter 9 of *Self-Regulation in the Classroom: Helping Students Learn How to Learn.*

INTERVIEWS

Interviewing is a method for reflecting that can also include practice of active and empathic listening skills. If students are reflecting individually, they can interview themselves about the lesson or activity. In groups, they can interview each other. Here are some good interview questions for reflection:

- What did you learn about yourself throughout this activity?
- How might you use your new learning in another content area?
- Which part of the activity was most challenging? Why?
- Which part of the activity was the most fun? Why?
- Which part of the activity was easy for you?
- How much did this activity help you make deeper meaning of the content?
- What do you plan to do better next time?
- How did you feel throughout the activity and why?
- How do you feel now that the activity is over and why?

QUESTIONING

Students can ask themselves or their group members questions about how the learning or activity went. Different from interviewing, this strategy requires everyone to actively engage in asking and answering questions, making it more like a conversation. Students may use the interviewing questions above to start.

JOURNALING

Students can reflect by journaling about their learning journey, including processing their thoughts, emotional responses, and actions. Reflecting through writing allows students to return to the past and gain a greater awareness of their personal and academic growth. When reflecting with a group, students can first journal on their own and then share their journals with peers.

LETTER WRITING

As a way to reflect on learning, students can write letters to themselves about how the lesson or activity went. They might write about who they were before the learning, who they are on the other side of it, and who they want to be in the future. Students may also consider writing to someone special (such as a friend or relative), sharing the ways they are growing as a learner. For group reflection, students can each write a letter to a peer about what to expect and what they'll learn in the lesson or activity and then discuss each other's letters.

JIGSAWS

Individually, students summarize in one sentence what they learned from the lesson or activity. They can share their sentence with a group of peers, highlighting any ideas that are repeated. The intent of jigsaws is to build a collection of strategies that worked or didn't work, acknowledge that others struggle with similar situations, and help students identify the main point of an activity.

QUIZ/TEST REFLECTIONS

After receiving a graded quiz or test, students review where they did well and where they need to focus their attention. They then write themselves a note or save the test or quiz with their reflections for future reference.

For group reflection, lead the group through the quiz or test to see where errors were commonly made, where misunderstandings happened, or where the information or questions were not clear. On a large piece of chart paper, record what the group should focus on in the next learning session. Keep the record posted somewhere in the classroom or make it virtual so students can store it in a special folder on their devices.

THINK-WRITE-PAIR-SHARE

Think-Write-Pair-Share is another reflection method that is easy to work into your schedule for the day or class period and includes both individual and group reflection. Invite students to spend a few moments by themselves thinking about what they learned. Then, using the Sentence Starters on page 159, have them spend one minute writing about their thoughts. Consider having students respond to at least one of the sentence starters from each of the ABC columns. Next, have students meet in pairs or small groups to share their ideas before sharing out with the larger group.

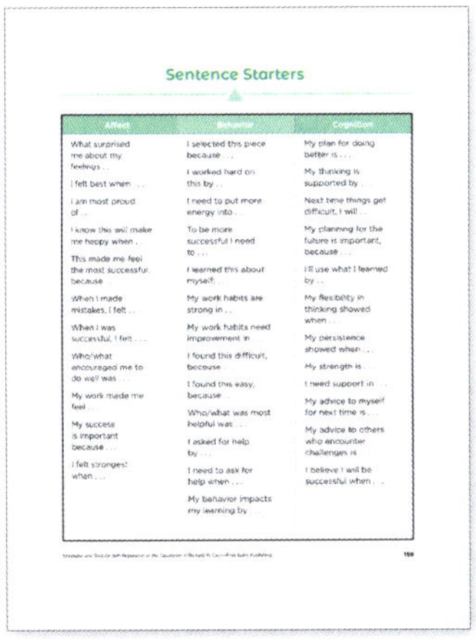

SHOUT-OUTS

Shout-outs (page 9) can be wonderful for reflecting on learning. To adapt the method for reflection, focus the shout-outs on how others' actions or support led to individual growth in a student's affect, behavior, and cognition.

PLUS/MINUS/DELTA

In this method of reflection, students describe their positive experiences in learning, their more challenging experiences, and what they would change in future learning experiences. Individually, they can create their own Plus/Minus/Delta on the lesson or activity using the prompts on page 160. They could also do this reflection in pairs or small groups, or with you in a large group.

This reflective method is also a powerful formative assessment tool for you to identify what students did well, how you might change an activity to be more engaging, and the depths to which students grasped the meaning of your instruction. It can also provide you with helpful information about what needs reteaching or enrichment.

ANALOGY REFLECTION STORYBOARD

Analogies relate one thing to something else and may help students connect abstract concepts or thoughts to concrete and perceivable images. In this way, they are an effective method for reflecting on learning.

Process:

1. Using a simple three-panel storyboard (page 161), have students sketch or write out simple statements about their affect, behavior, and cognition in learning. You can show the example below if students need help getting started.

Affect: I feel . . .	Behavior: I do . . .	Cognition: I think . . .
I feel like I'm tangled in weeds in mathematics.	I work as hard as a steam engine in this class.	My plan is to be focused like a microscope during this next unit.

2. Students can share their storyboards with their study buddies or in small groups. They can hold onto their sketches as a way to stay aware of where they have been and how they are growing personally and academically.

Reward, Relax, Recharge

Congratulations to you and your students! Making it to the fourth phase of learning means it is time to celebrate students' accomplishments, no matter how big or how small, to set their confidence to begin the next learning process. Now is the time to solidify for students the connection between hard work and success—between effort and achievement. It is also a time to consider any lessons learned along the way.

Too often, teaching and learning are focused on correcting mistakes, calling out errors, and pointing toward the "right" answer. Feedback is mostly in the form of what needs attention or correction. For students to build positive self-belief (cognition), feel a sense of self-efficacy (affect), and be able to apply what they learned to the future (behavior), they must feel good about their accomplishments and know that the strategies they are learning are meaningful.

Little research has been focused on celebrating student success. However, we do know that recognition by teachers and others can have a tremendous positive impact on students. The pressure to excel academically, participate in extracurricular activities, and navigate social dynamics can be overwhelming for students. Teaching them to relax and reward themselves can have positive effects on their physical and mental well-being and academic success. For self-regulated learners, celebrating is about rewarding the general qualities that led to success, relaxing once the mountain has been conquered, and recharging their confidence for the next learning event. This section includes strategies and tools to help students do just that.

Strategies for Teachers

Teachers play an important role in students' lives. Many successful people cite a favorite teacher who celebrated their talents and encouraged their growth. Below are some ways you can reward your students' successes and help them relax and recharge for the learning ahead.

GIVE DESCRIPTIVE AND POSITIVE FEEDBACK

Feedback comes in many forms, from classroom discussions to quizzes to standardized assessments. Refocusing feedback from punitive (what a student did wrong) to affirmative (what a student is doing well) has a significant effect on student learning, motivation, and mental health. When commenting on student work, boost students' self-esteem by framing feedback through growth mindset statements:

- "Your work is showing great improvement."
- "Even though you have errors, I can see you are trying your best."
- "I'm most impressed by how hard you work at doing a good job."
- "When you put your mind to it, you can do almost anything."
- "I can see that you kept your focus on the right things."

COMMUNICATE WITH HOME

Parents and guardians love to hear good things about their children. You can send notes home or call, text, or email the good news about students on a routine basis. While you'll occasionally have to discuss issues with families, be sure that your first contact home is positive to set you up for building strong and supportive relationships.

Celebration Tunnel

Have students stand in two rows facing each other. Each student raises their arms and holds hands with the student across from them to create a tunnel. Students who are being celebrated run through the tunnel as the class cheers them on.

DISPLAY EXCEPTIONAL WORK

Create a space the bulletin board or wall space with the header of "EXCEPTIONAL." Work that exceeds expectations and shows exceptional quality is published here. This highlights the work as being a superior representation of hard work and effort. This display is not meant to be a showcase for all student work. It is for those students who have worked hard, who show exceptional growth, and who rose above the expectations.

INVITE VISITORS IN TO CELEBRATE

Asking the school principal, superintendent, school board members, mayor, city council members, or local businesspeople to join your class in celebrating student success can be powerful. Have students share their challenges and how they rose above them with visitors. These visits are special occasions. Use them when students meet a major accomplishment or complete an involved project.

CREATE TIME FOR YOURSELF

All too often, teachers spend enormous amounts of time planning and preparing for students. One way to decrease stress and take care of you is to block out time in the day that is just for you. This can be time before, during, or after school. During this time, it is important to try to detach from devices. You might read a good book, close your eyes, or recline in your favorite chair. Share with students how you carve out this time in your day.

BREATHE

Most people do not do a very good job of breathing, especially when they get busy or stressed. Taking intentional deep breaths is a great way to relax the mind and body to prepare for what's ahead. Share this deep-breathing exercise with students:

1. Slowly breathe in through the nose while counting to four.
2. Hold the breath for another four seconds.
3. Exhale slowly for four seconds through the mouth.
4. Repeat three more times.

SHARE YOUR OWN WELL-BEING EFFORTS

Modeling healthy behaviors for your students goes a long way. It will not only encourage them to maintain a healthy lifestyle, but it can also encourage you to stay healthy as well. See the strategies on pages 36–42 in part I for ideas.

SET A STANDARD OF COURTESY AND RESPECT

When the learning environment is pleasant, free of fear, and welcoming to all, stress and anxiety are greatly diminished. See pages 7–15 in part I for strategies to create a welcoming and supportive classroom.

Techniques and Tools for Students

Share these ideas for how students can reward themselves for their learning and effort and relax and recharge for the next learning challenge.

REWARD

As a teacher, you can (and should!) reward students for their hard work and success in the classroom. But for students to become self-regulated learners, they must also learn how to reward themselves and celebrate their peers. Any time a student feels they have reached a major success point is a time when they can reward themself—this might be when they successfully complete a project or activity, when they have overcome a hurdle, or when they have accomplished a goal. They can celebrate these same milestones for their peers.

Share these ideas:

- **Treat yourself.** Upon successful completion of an activity or project, students can reward themselves with something they find motivating. This could include a bit of time on a social media account, playing a favorite game, doing a favorite activity, or having a favorite treat.
- **Recognize others through a "Learning Support Award."** Students can give this award to someone who was supportive of or assisted them throughout their learning. They can use the award to express their appreciation for how the person helped them attain success.
- **Write a thank-you note.** If students don't feel comfortable giving an award, they can simply write a note to express how someone positively impacted their learning.
- **Plan a small-group activity with study partners.** This can be done during school hours (such as lunching together, playing a group game at recess, or asking the teacher for some free time to meet as a group) or before or after school (such as a breakfast, game night, or pizza dinner together). There is no need to have a structure during this time—the point is to enjoy each other's company.
- **Share successes with others.** Students might write notes to parents or caregivers telling these adults about their accomplishments in learning. They could also text a friend or post on social media the pride they have in their hard work.

RELAX AND RECHARGE

Self-regulated learners understand that learning is often hard work and that effort is the key to success. They also know it is difficult to keep striving if they never let themselves relax. Share these ideas with students for how they can relax and recharge for the next challenge to come:

- **Exercise.** As described in the section on health and well-being in part I, exercise is not only beneficial to overall health, but also a great way to relax and recharge after challenging situations. Encourage students to spend at least twenty minutes three times a week doing some sort of exercise.
- **Take a rest.** A brief downtime, between fifteen and thirty minutes, is a wonderful way to relax and recharge one's battery. Students can use this time to nap, listen to music, practice deep breathing or another calming strategy, or simply tune out the world. Remind students that it is essential to "disconnect" from devices during this time.
- **Read for fun.** Whether students are reading an epic fantasy or a funny comic, reading is a powerful way to reduce stress and recharge energy. Encourage students to spend at least twenty minutes every day reading something they enjoy.

- **Work on a puzzle.** Another way students can let go of stress and anxiety is to lose themselves in a complex puzzle. Puzzles with lots of color and multiple pieces are best. They might also enjoy word puzzles, logic puzzles, or mystery puzzles as ways to destress and recharge.
- **Do yoga or stretching.** Not only are yoga and stretching good for flexibility, strength, and balance, but they can also alleviate stress, muscle fatigue, headaches, and other ailments. Students can use yoga and stretching to clear their minds of negative thoughts and improve their mood and sleep.

THE 3-3-3 RULE

This activity can help center students, decrease their anxiety, and increase their personal awareness. Guide students through the process a few times and then invite them to use this tool whenever they need a moment to relax and recharge. This activity can be done at the beginning of a class period, before taking a test, or in preparation for a difficult task as a way for students to center themselves, focus, and reduce anxiety. When doing this exercise, students can keep their thoughts to themselves or share in a small-group or whole-class discussion.

Process:

1. Direct students to look around their space and select three things they can see, three things they can hear, and three things they can touch.
2. Ask students to think about the three things they can see:
   - What colors/shapes are they?
   - What emotions do they bring up in you?
   - What makes them interesting or unique?
3. Ask students to think about the three things they can hear:
   - How high or low is the pitch?
   - What emotions do the sounds bring up in you?
   - What makes the sounds interesting or unique?
4. Ask students to think about the three things they can touch:
   - How do they feel?
   - What emotions do the sensations bring up in you?
   - What makes the sensations interesting or unique?
5. Prompt students to take three deep breaths.

Appendix: Student Pages

For digital versions of these resources, see page 175.

50 Affirmations to Try

1. I can do this.
2. I am confident in myself.
3. I am proud of who I've become.
4. I have the right to be happy.
5. I am powerful.
6. I am strong.
7. I get better each time I try.
8. I am an unstoppable force.
9. I inspire others to do better.
10. I may fail, but I learn each time.
11. I haven't done XYZ yet, but eventually I will.
12. My attitude is contagious. I hope others catch my good vibes.
13. My joy/happiness is worth passing along to others.
14. I work hard to achieve success.
15. I will stay focused on my success.
16. I've overcome obstacles in the past. I can do it this time too.
17. My hard work will show in my achievements.
18. Each day, I get better and better.
19. I believe in myself.
20. I can do almost anything I put my mind to.
21. I am freeing myself from negative thoughts.
22. I accept who I am, and I will continue to do great things.
23. I deserve to be happy/successful.
24. I have made mistakes, but they don't define me.
25. I like myself the way I am.
26. I choose happiness
27. Struggles make me stronger.
28. I am a strong and capable person.
29. It may be hard, but it's worth the challenge.
30. I am allowed to be sad, mad, or unhappy. It's part of being human.
31. I am allowed to be happy.
32. I can set boundaries without feeling bad about it.
33. I am worthy of praise and support.
34. The past is the past. Today is a new beginning.
35. I matter.
36. Growth can be difficult, but I'm getting better every day.
37. When I get stressed, I can remember to breathe.
38. I'm not bored. I'm waiting for inspiration.
39. I will avoid distractions during XYZ.
40. I work hard to be my best self.
41. Even though I may not win, I will do my best.
42. My feelings are mine. I will remain positive through difficult feelings.
43. Each breath gives me peace/strength/power.
44. I live in the moment.
45. I am grateful for all the things I have.
46. I am filled with joy.
47. I greet challenges with gratitude.
48. Today, I choose to be happy.
49. I embrace my uniqueness, because there is no one like me!
50. I can do hard things.

Daily Schedule

Name: ______________________________ Date: ______________

❍ S ❍ M ❍ T ❍ W ❍ Th ❍ F ❍ S

Today's Schedule	
6–7 a.m.	Today's Goal
7–8 a.m.	
8–9 a.m.	Priorities
9–10 a.m.	
10–11 a.m.	
11–noon	
noon–1 p.m.	
1–2 p.m.	
2–3 p.m.	
3–4 p.m.	To-Do List
4–5 p.m.	
5–6 p.m.	
6–7 p.m.	
7–8 p.m.	
8–9 p.m.	
9–10 p.m.	

Weekly Schedule

Name: ______________________ Date: ______________

	Sunday	Monday	Tuesday	Wednesday	Thursday	Friday	Saturday
Before School							
At School							
After School							

Student Learning Survey

Name: ______________________________ Date: ______________

Check all the statements that are true for you.

Paper Clip

- ☐ I like to have a timeline for doing work.
- ☐ I am most comfortable doing things by myself.
- ☐ I like to keep myself organized.
- ☐ I feel best when I accomplish a task completely.
- ☐ I like to make lists of what needs to be done.
- ☐ I believe it is important to follow rules and directions.
- ☐ I feel frustrated when I don't know the right answer.
- ☐ I like to do things that are step-by-step.
- ☐ I work best when I know what is expected.

If you agree with a majority of these statements, you may be considered a "paper clip" type of learner.

As a paper clip, you feel comfortable with:

- schedules and deadlines
- knowing what is going to happen and when it will happen
- organization
- step-by-step directions

As a paper clip, you may need support with:

- dealing with changes to the schedule
- not knowing what is coming next
- disorganization
- random tasks

Student Learning Survey (continued)

Name: ______________________________ Date: ____________________

Check all the statements that are true for you.

Teddy Bear

- ☐ I know how I feel and recognize how others feel.
- ☐ I work best with others on projects and tasks.
- ☐ I like to make others feel good about themselves.
- ☐ I enjoy making things and doing things for others.
- ☐ It's important for me to make connections to topics I am learning.
- ☐ I work best when my group partners agree.
- ☐ I like problems that are real and can have real consequences.
- ☐ I believe I am an ethical person.
- ☐ I like to help others complete tasks.

If you agree with a majority of these statements, you may be considered a "teddy bear" type of learner.

As a teddy bear, you feel comfortable with:

- understanding others' feelings
- working in groups
- dealing with authentic problems
- helping others be their best

As a teddy bear, you may need support with:

- doing things on you own
- dealing with adversity
- working through novel (or unreal) activities
- debating points of view

continued ➡

Student Learning Survey (continued)

Name: ______________________________ Date: ______________

Check all the statements that are true for you.

Magnifying Glass

- ☐ I like to see the big picture when I'm learning something new.
- ☐ I enjoy investigating problems and then trying to solve those problems.
- ☐ I work best on my own.
- ☐ I feel it is healthy to debate points of view with others.
- ☐ I like to ask questions for clarity.
- ☐ I enjoy when decisions can be made.
- ☐ I believe it is okay to disagree with others' decisions and opinions.
- ☐ I am good at analyzing what others think.
- ☐ I like to do things in an ordered way.

If you agree with a majority of these statements, you may be considered a "magnifying glass" type of learner.

As a magnifying glass, you feel comfortable with:

- seeing the entire picture before making a decision
- complex problems that need solving
- coming up with your own opinion about situations
- taking time to think about solutions

As a magnifying glass, you may need support with:

- understanding the emotional reactions of others
- listening to others' ideas
- making a decision with other people
- working through problems that don't have an easy answer

Student Learning Survey (continued)

Name: ____________________ Date: ____________

Check all the statements that are true for you.

Slinky

- ❑ I enjoy coming up with new ideas.
- ❑ I like to move around when I'm thinking.
- ❑ I like to do things in different ways.
- ❑ I work best with others who think like I do.
- ❑ I like to express myself in many different ways.
- ❑ I like to talk with others about my ideas.
- ❑ I enjoy situations where there may be many answers to consider.
- ❑ I can make up stories or situations easily.
- ❑ I often come up with answers quickly.

If you agree with a majority of these statements, you may be considered a "slinky" type of learner.

As a slinky, you feel comfortable with:

- new ideas or out-of-the-box suggestions
- coming up with your own way to do things
- expressing yourself in a variety of ways
- imagining what is possible

As a slinky, you may need support with:

- waiting your turn
- listening to others
- taking time to think before answering
- meeting deadlines

Personal Learning Plan

Name: ______________________________ Date: ______________

Who do I want to be?	
How does this class help?	
What do I need to do?	
What are the hurdles?	
How will I overcome those hurdles?	
Who is my goal buddy?	Goal buddy's signature

Created by Katharine McCoy, math teacher, Bishop DuBourg HS, St. Louis, MO. Used with permission.

Organizing Learning Space Checklist

Name: ______________________________ Date: ______________

- ❑ My space is free from clutter (unnecessary papers, books, visual distractions).
- ❑ Distractions are at a minimum.
  - ❑ My phone is on do not disturb or silent.
  - ❑ Music is low and calming.
  - ❑ Others know not to bother me during my learning time.
- ❑ My workspace is comfortable.
- ❑ I understand what is expected of me during my study time.
- ❑ The materials I need are close at hand and organized.
- ❑ I can quickly find help if I need it (whether it be a person or website).
- ❑ I have set a timer for when to take a break (breaks should last no more than 5–10 minutes).
- ❑ I have set a timer for my work time.
- ❑ I have set my reward for when I complete my work time.

Eisenhower Matrix for Managing and Prioritizing Tasks

Name: ______________________________ Date: ______________

	Urgent	Not Urgent
Important	*For example, assignment is due tomorrow*	*For example, assignment is due at the end of the week*
Not Important	*For example, interruptions from a friend seeking help or advice on a noncritical matter*	*For example, interruptions from a friend sharing a fun video or asking what you are doing this weekend*

The exact origin of this matrix has not been identified but is attributed to the leadership lessons from the life of Dwight D. Eisenhower.

Assignment Checklist

Name: ______________________________ Date: ____________________

Assignment Description	Due Date	Midway Due Date	Expectations/ Objectives	Potential Obstacles	Remedies

Priority Ladder

Name: ______________________________ Date: ______________

Issue:	MOST IMPORTANT
	LEAST IMPORTANT

Symptoms of Stress

Name: ______________________________ Date: ______________

Watch for these signs of stress. If they appear for prolonged periods of time, seek help from a parent, teacher, counselor, or other trusted adult.

Affective: If you . . .

- lack a sense of joy or happiness
- have a negative attitude or behaviors
- approach schoolwork with resentment or resignation
- express boredom
- become easily agitated, frustrated, or moody
- feel overwhelmed or out of control
- have low self-esteem
- feel worthless
- feel depressed

Behavioral: If you . . .

- have sleep issues
- procrastinate or avoid responsibilities
- overreact to normal or simple situations
- suffer fatigue, low energy, chronic tiredness
- have nervous habits (bite nails, chew on lips/clothes, pick at self)
- suffer frequent physical ailments such as headaches or stomachaches
- experience colds or other sicknesses often
- exhibit increasing neediness or clinging behaviors
- avoid being with others
- experience muscle tension or tightness

Cognition: If you . . .

- are unable to get or stay focused
- have disorganized thinking
- lost perspective on normal or simple situations
- are unable to "quiet your mind"
- worry continually
- have racing thoughts
- make poor decisions
- have constant negative thoughts

Being Healthy Bingo

Name: ______________________________ Date: ______________

Ate at least 3 vegetables in one day	Ate at least 2 fruits in one day	Increased physical activity from one day to the next	Took at least 5 deep breaths in one day	Had a "phone free" day
Eliminated my screen time at least 2 hours before bedtime	Read for at least 20 minutes 1–3 times in a week	Journaled about my feelings or my day	Talked face-to-face with a friend about my feelings or my day	Read for at least 20 minutes 5 days in one week
Took a short nap	Danced to my favorite song	FREE SPACE	Told a friend 3 things I appreciate about them	Complimented a stranger
Listened to the sounds of nature	Completed my schoolwork on time	Called a friend	Asked for help	Got a good night's sleep
Stretched in the morning or before bed	Organized my space	Helped someone	Took time for myself	Learned something new

SMARTS/S Goal-Setting

Name: ______________________ Date: ______________

Specific	Ask yourself: What do I want to achieve?
Measurable	Ask yourself: How will I know when I've reached my goal?
Achievable	Ask yourself: How can I make my goal "just right"?
Relevant	Ask yourself: How does this goal support my other goals?
Time-Based	Ask yourself: When will my goal be accomplished?
Strategies to Success	Ask yourself: How will my goal help me succeed?

My SMARTS/S Goal:

D3R Goal Setting

Name: ______________________________ Date: ______________

Define	Refine
(What is my goal?)	(What do I need to achieve my goal?)
Reward	**Reflect**
(What will I do to motivate myself to work through obstacles?)	(How will I know I've met my goal?)

TSAP

Name: ______________________________ Date: ______________

Term	Synonyms	Antonyms	Positive Plan
Procrastination (example)	avoid, delay, hesitate, linger, wait	act, do, finish, go, persist	To avoid procrastinating, I will set a plan to act and finish my work on time.
Reluctance			
Fear			
Distractions			
Bias			

Tips to Stay Focused

Take a mental break. Studying is a taxing process for the brain. When studying or learning something new, try to take a two-minute break for every ten minutes of focused work.

Avoid distractions, such as your phone, while studying. If your home is noisy, try to move yourself to a quiet space.

Go back over your notes to see what you are missing, what you remember, or what you find interesting about the topic at hand.

Go for a quick walk. If you need to move during class and can't get up to walk, you can still do small physical movements. Bouncing your legs under your desk, doing small calf raises, or taking a deep breath are all ways to keep your brain active.

Talk to your teacher if you feel that the lecture or parts of the lesson go long. Be sure to do this in private and be respectful. Simply state the fact that you are finding yourself having a hard time staying focused during long stretches of the lesson and ask for a small break to gather your thoughts or get up and stretch. This will likely benefit everyone in your class.

Make sure your space is organized and free of clutter. Disorganized and cluttered spaces may cause your brain to feel disorganized and cluttered as well.

Be sure to eat well, exercise, and get enough sleep. Your diet and amount of activity and sleep you get can affect your focus and attention.

Practice mindfulness or meditation strategies or seek support if you feel you have too many thoughts going on in your head.

Get outdoors. In school or at home, one of the best places to take a break is in a natural environment. A natural environment might be a park or any other natural setting. If you're in class and can't go outside, look out the windows or find nature wherever you can, even if it's just a plant in the room. Focus on the nature, look at the colors and design, and let wonder fill your mind.

Train your brain to focus for longer periods of time. The natural default mode of your brain is to wander and daydream. Of course, daydreaming is not bad. In the classroom, mind-wandering can affect your academic performance. A way to train your brain to stay attentive for longer periods of time is to use concentration exercises. These can include card games, reading a difficult passage from a novel very slowly, listening to a favorite podcast, playing a skip counting game, doing a crossword puzzle, or listing your favorite foods in alphabetical order. Be sure to practice training your brain on a daily basis, several times a day.

Study Q&A

Q: When is the best time to study?

A: The optimal time to study depends on your natural patterns of activity and sleep.

- **Morning study time** may be beneficial if you have had a good night's sleep. The brain tends to be sharpest in the morning, especially after a good breakfast. In addition, the natural sunlight is good for your eyes and for gaining vitamin D. You can use morning study time to learn something new or review notes from the day before.
- **Afternoon study time** is a time for the brain to integrate new information with what you already know. Since this is the time after school, you can use it to reflect on what you have learned throughout the day and what you remember. It's also a good time to connect with peers in a study group or to contact someone who can help you when you get stuck. Plus, libraries will be open if you need more information.
- **Night study time** is generally not the most effective time to learn. Based on how you feel at the end of the day, you may be more likely to concentrate on difficult content at night or it may be best to leave it for the next day.

Q: How long should I study?

A: You are the best judge of your own concentration and how much energy you have available. But, in general, follow the ten-minute rule. Try to study for ten minutes per your grade level each night. For example:

- Third grade: 30 minutes
- Fourth grade: 40 minutes
- Fifth grade: 50 minutes
- Middle school (grades 6–8): 60 minutes
- High school (grades 9–12): 90 to 120 minutes

Q: What if I need to work longer than the ten-minute rule?

A: Some research suggests that doing more may actually be doing less. A study by the Stanford Graduate School of Education found that students in some of the highest performing high schools who spent more than 120 minutes studying did not gain greater academic success. In fact, some students who did more than three hours of homework "experienced . . .more academic stress, physical health problems, and lack of balance in their lives" (Galloway, Conner, and Pope 2013, 490).

continued ➡

Study Q&A (continued)

Q: What can I do to keep focused?

A: It's natural for your mind to wander when studying. To stay focused, try these tips:

- take a break
- avoid distractions
- review notes
- keep your space organized
- take care of your physical needs (such as eating when hungry and drinking when thirsty)

Q: What should I do when I need to reset?

A: Sometimes, you may find yourself heading in the wrong direction, making multiple mistakes, feeling overwhelmed or bored, or simply not understanding what to do next. This is an indication that it's time to take a step back.

One way to do this is to stop what you are doing and do something different for about ten minutes. You might go for a walk, exercise, make a snack, read a book, play some music, or play a quick game on your phone. Try to avoid opening social media or email, though, as they can be major distractions.

Chronotype Survey

Name: ______________________________ Date: ______________

Read the statements for each of the chronotypes. Check all the statements that are true for you. If you check a majority of one of the chronotype's characteristics, you may fall into that category.

Wolf

- ☐ I have trouble waking up in the morning.
- ☐ I feel most productive between noon and 4 p.m.
- ☐ I get a boost of energy later in the day.
- ☐ I am a "night owl." I don't get tired until very late.
- ☐ I tend to be one of the last people to leave a party.
- ☐ I don't like to eat a lot in the morning, but I'm very hungry in the afternoon.
- ☐ I'm not much into exercise.
- ☐ I most like to spend time with friends and family in the evening or at night.

Bear

- ☐ I tend to wake up around the time the sun rises.
- ☐ I like to nap in the afternoon.
- ☐ I like to go to bed around 11 p.m., after spending a few hours unwinding.
- ☐ I like to exercise early in the morning or in the late afternoon.
- ☐ I get the most done in the earlier part of the day.
- ☐ I don't like to be alone too much.
- ☐ I am hungry in the morning and don't like to skip breakfast.
- ☐ I most like to spend time with friends and family in the afternoon and early evening.

continued ➡

Breus, Michael. 2024a. "Chronotypes." Sleep Doctor. Updated January 29, 2024. sleepdoctor.com/pages/chronotypes.

Chronotype Survey (continued)

Dolphin

- ❑ I tend to be a light sleeper.
- ❑ I have a hard time sticking to a schedule for going to bed and waking up.
- ❑ I often feel slow or dazed in the morning.
- ❑ I find it hard to "turn off" my brain while falling asleep.
- ❑ I don't tend to relax in the evening.
- ❑ I have an active mind throughout the day. My brain seems to be "on" all the time.
- ❑ I feel most alert in the late afternoon.
- ❑ I most like to spend time with friends and family in the evening.

Lion

- ❑ I enjoy waking up early. I am a morning person.
- ❑ I have a lot of energy early in the day.
- ❑ I tend to go to bed early.
- ❑ I am driven to get things done.
- ❑ I enjoy being active early in the morning.
- ❑ I like to take naps in the afternoon.
- ❑ I most like to spend time with friends and family in the morning.
- ❑ I start to feel impatient and cranky in the late afternoon.

Breus, Michael. 2024a. "Chronotypes." Sleep Doctor. Updated January 29, 2024. sleepdoctor.com/pages/chronotypes.

Chronotype Tips

Now that you know your chronotype, look over the following strategies. These can help you be more effective during your day and efficient with your use of time.

9 Strategies for Wolves

Wolves might also be called "night owls." They like to stay up late and have bursts of energy later in the day.

1. Set at least two alarms to help you wake up in the morning.
2. Try not to sleep in later than 8 a.m., as sleeping in can make it difficult to go to bed at night.
3. Avoid taking naps, as they can challenge your nighttime sleep.
4. Since mornings may be difficult, use morning time to plan out your day and get organized.
5. Try to schedule your most energy-consuming or challenging activities for the afternoon.
6. It's okay to do your homework or study later in the evening.
7. It's best for you to exercise later in the day, between 6 and 9 p.m.
8. Avoid drinking caffeinated beverages after 2 p.m.
9. Eat a balanced lunch in the afternoon and delay your dinner until around 8 p.m. This will help you sleep better at night.

9 Strategies for Bears

Bears are the most common chronotype, making up about 55 percent of the population. They like to get a full eight hours of sleep and are most productive in the morning and early afternoon.

1. It's okay to hit the snooze button, but be sure to get up by 8 a.m.
2. Since your energy will decline in the afternoon, take a nap (between 20 and 40 minutes).
3. Be sure to take some time in the evening to wind down from your day. This will help you fall asleep faster.
4. Plan and organize your day so that you are doing the most energy-consuming and challenging activities between 10 a.m. and 12 p.m.
5. Your best time to study is late afternoon into early evening.

continued ➡

Breus, Michael. 2024a. "Chronotypes." Sleep Doctor. Updated January 29, 2024. sleepdoctor.com/pages/chronotypes.

Chronotype Tips (continued)

6. It's best for you to exercise early in the morning or in the late afternoon.
7. Your biggest meal of the day should be breakfast, and you can consume caffeine in the morning.
8. Eat a balanced lunch in the afternoon and enjoy a snack around 4 p.m. to keep your energy up.
9. Your smallest meal of the day should be dinner. Try to eat no later than 8 p.m.

9 Strategies for Dolphins

Dolphins are light sleepers and often don't get a consistent full night's sleep. They also are very sensitive to noise, especially at night. Dolphins are most productive at midday.

1. Don't worry if you don't sleep through the night like others—you have a low sleep drive.
2. Avoid taking naps, as they will disrupt your sleep patterns even more.
3. Try not to go to bed too early, as this may cause you to toss and turn.
4. Avoid lounging and watching TV in bed, as this can turn your brain up!
5. Be sure to keep your bedroom dark, quiet, and cool for a better night's sleep.
6. Since you may start the early part of your day in a daze, use this time to gather your thoughts, organize your day, and slowly get into your routine.
7. The best time for energy-consuming and challenging tasks is late morning or late afternoon.
8. To clear your brain after school or study, do something you enjoy that helps you decompress.
9. Be sure to drink a lot of water throughout the day.

Breus, Michael. 2024a. "Chronotypes." Sleep Doctor. Updated January 29, 2024. sleepdoctor.com/pages/chronotypes.

Chronotype Tips (continued)

9 Strategies for Lions

Lions are early birds. They wake up before the sun and are most productive in the morning. Their hard work during the day puts them to bed at a reasonable hour.

1. It's best for you to do your energy-consuming and challenging tasks early in the day.
2. You will do your best thinking and planning early in the day.
3. It's okay to take a nap in the middle of the day.
4. Avoid screen time before bed.
5. To avoid the afternoon slump, go for a walk, drink a caffeinated drink, or go to lunch with friends.
6. Use afternoon time for less taxing tasks or just to do some thinking.
7. Due to your sleep patterns, it is best to do your socializing late in the afternoon or early in the evening.
8. Eat a high-protein, low-carb breakfast, a mid-morning snack, a healthy lunch, and a carb-heavy dinner.
9. Stretch or do yoga in the morning, but save more strenuous exercise for the afternoon. This will help with the afternoon slump.

Breus, Michael. 2024a. "Chronotypes." Sleep Doctor. Updated January 29, 2024. sleepdoctor.com/pages/chronotypes.

Note-Taking with Picture and Words

Name: ______________________ Date: ______________

Draw	
Write	__________ __________ __________ __________ __________ __________ __________ __________ __________ __________

Note-Taking Organizer

Name: ______________________________ Date: ______________

Key Words	Unfamiliar Words
› ________	› ________
› ________	› ________
› ________	› ________
› ________	› ________
› ________	› ________

Thinking Images	My Key Points (Jot your ideas.)
	› ________
	› ________
	› ________
	› ________
	› ________

Write	Summary
________	________
________	________
________	________
________	________
________	________

Cornell Notes

Name: ______________________________ Date: ______________

Topic: ______________________________

SECTION 2: Cues	SECTION 1: Notes

SECTION 3: Summary

What? So What? Now What?

Name: ______________________________ Date: ________________

What? (Translation)	So What? (Interpretation)	Now What? (Extrapolation)

Spider Diagram

Name: ______________________________ Date: ______________

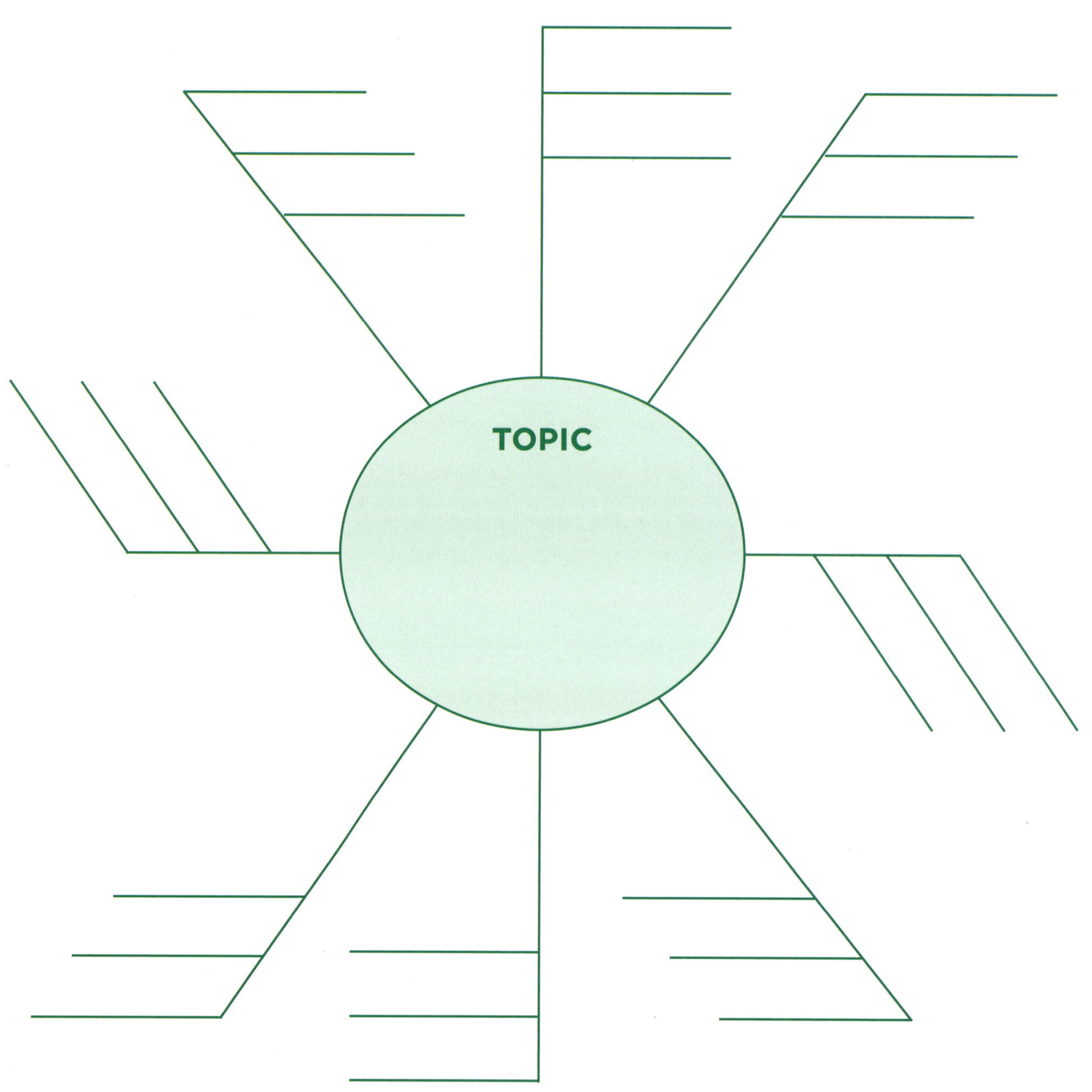

Note-Taking Tips

Listen for important details.

Don't try to get every word down. Instead, try to focus on the big ideas or those words or phrases that keep getting repeated.

Do make sure to write down anything the teacher writes on the board or projection—this usually means it's important.

Put a star ★ in front of important information. This includes anything the teacher tells you is important and anything written on the board or projection.

Review your notes soon after class. You can do this as a home study practice or before the next class session. Reviewing your notes is even more important than taking notes.

Ask questions. If something doesn't make sense or you have a question, don't be afraid to ask for clarification. If you run out of time to ask questions, jot them down in the margins of your notes to remind you to ask before or after class.

Leave the last few pages of your notebook blank. This will come in handy when ideas, questions, or topics come up that you may want to investigate later.

Don't stop taking notes until the class time is completely over. You may miss something important when you are packing up early.

Tips for Avoiding Distractions

Know yourself as a learner. Identify the way you learn best, whether that's through reading information, listening to new ideas, or doing activities that help you make sense of a topic. Knowing how you like to learn helps you when it comes to focusing on and completing a task with little distraction.

Get your distractions out of the way before you start a project. Spend time upfront getting the distractions out of your system.

Think *won't* instead of *can't*. Don't think about a tempting distraction as something you can't do. Think of it as something that you won't do. Can't thinking, such as *I can't text my friends while I'm studying,* is "out-of-control" thinking, which means that you take no responsibilities for your actions. Won't thinking (*I won't text my friends while I'm studying*) means you are in control of your actions and thoughts.

Set a time during the day where there will be NO distractions—shut down social media, eliminate texting, and only use the internet for research or idea generation.

Get a study buddy who will help you stay on task. Choose this person wisely; you want to make sure this person can also avoid distractions.

Outline, make a schedule, or use a planner to decide what needs to be done. Put time limitations on the work you are doing.

From your outline, **schedule or create a prioritized list.** Do one thing at a time. Plus, decide whether everything needs to be done today or whether some things can wait until the next study period.

Make time to be distracted. For every hour of focus, give yourself five to ten minutes to engage in texting or social media (if this limit is realistic for you!).

Frequently change where you study to provide a fresh outlook on thinking and learning. Studies show that when we routinely change our positions, we actually remember more when we are in the new setting.

List and then eliminate things that are potentially distracting. You may have to put your phone in another room, turn off the music, or tell your friends you are not available from 8 a.m. until noon. Clean up your space to make it free of the distractions.

Tips for Avoiding Distractions (continued)

Know how to get back on track after a distraction. Some things can't be ignored, such as a fire drill or announcement interruptions. Take a moment to breathe and then refocus.

When you do get distracted, **adjust your time frame to accommodate for the distraction**. If you spent five minutes texting your friend in the middle of a task, then expand your study time by five minutes. Don't look at it as a punishment but rather as an adjustment you can control.

Don't allow others to control your focus. Avoid sitting with or near students who may not be as well-regulated as you would like to be or are. Don't let them bother you. If they do, seek assistance from the teacher in adjusting your situation.

Reward yourself when you have met your goal. If you plan for a 50-minute period of distraction-free work time and you make it, give yourself a reward of doing something fun, or simply go on social media to tell others of your accomplishments.

Learning Log

Name: ______________________________ Date: ________________

Date	Activity	What I did	How I felt about it	My plan for next time

KIQ Chart

Name: ______________________________ Date: ______________

What I KNOW about this topic	What I find INTERESTING about this topic	What I QUESTION or don't know about this topic

I Chart

Name: ______________________________ Date: ____________

I wonder	I discovered
I think	I question
I believe	I plan
I connected	I learned

What Interests Me: Topic Preview

Name: ______________________ Date: ______________

1. Write the title of the source material: ______________________

2. What do you think the title means? OR what are your thoughts on the title?

____

____

____

____

3. Look over the contents. List at least three headings that jump out at you.

____

____

____

4. Preview the entire source. Pick out three sections that seem interesting to you.

   › Section title: ______________________

   › Why I think it's interesting: ______________________

   › Questions I have about this section: ______________________

   ____

   ____

   ____

   › Section title: ______________________

   › Why I think it's interesting: ______________________

continued ➡

What Interests Me: Topic Preview (continued)

› Questions I have about this section: ______________________________

____

____

____

› Section title: ______________________________

› Why I think it's interesting: ______________________________

› Questions I have about this section: ______________________________

____

____

____

5. Find a textbook, a website, or another resource that is similar to the source material or that deals with the same topic. If possible, bring it to share with the class. Write the new source here: ______________________________

____

____

Personal Reflection

Name: ______________________________ Date: ______________

Date	What went well?	What needs improvement?	Who did I collaborate with?	What additional resources do I need?	What are my next steps?

For use with pages 106–107

Check Your Understanding

Name: ______________________________ Date: ______________

Studies show that dogs understand human emotions. They can read people's faces and voices. Dogs can even smell when a person is scared.

Sentence Starters

Affect	Behavior	Cognition
What surprised me about my feelings . . .	I selected this piece because . . .	My plan for doing better is . . .
I felt best when . . .	I worked hard on this by . . .	My thinking is supported by . . .
I am most proud of . . .	I need to put more energy into . . .	Next time things get difficult, I will . . .
I know this will make me happy when . . .	To be more successful I need to . . .	My planning for the future is important, because . . .
This made me feel the most successful, because . . .	I learned this about myself: . . .	I'll use what I learned by . . .
When I made mistakes, I felt . . .	My work habits are strong in . . .	My flexibility in thinking showed when . . .
When I was successful, I felt . . .	My work habits need improvement in . . .	My persistence showed when . . .
Who/what encouraged me to do well was . . .	I found this difficult, because . . .	My strength is . . .
My work made me feel . . .	I found this easy, because . . .	I need support in . . .
My success is important because . . .	Who/what was most helpful was . . .	My advice to myself for next time is . . .
I felt strongest when . . .	I asked for help by . . .	My advice to others who encounter challenges is . . .
	I need to ask for help when . . .	I believe I will be successful when . . .
	My behavior impacts my learning by . . .	

Plus/Minus/Delta Prompts

Plus	Minus	Delta (Change)
What I liked was . . . My positive feelings were . . . What went well was . . . What motivated me was . . . Who/what kept me going was . . . My positive thoughts were . . . How I grew was . . . How my responsibility increased was . . . How I can use this in the future is . . . What I will do again is . . .	What I didn't like was . . . My negative feelings were . . . What didn't go well was . . . What demotivated me was . . . Who/what distracted me was . . . How I did not grow was . . . How I lacked responsibility was . . . Why I won't do this the same way again is . . .	What I would change to make it better is . . . How I can reframe my feelings to feel better about this is . . . How I can get myself motivated is . . . What can keep me going is . . . What I can do to ensure I'm growing each time is . . . What I can do to strengthen my responsibilities to learn is . . . What I can do next time to increase my learning is . . .

Analogy Reflection Storyboard

Name: ______________________________ Date: ____________________

Affect: I feel . . .	Behavior: I do . . .	Cognition: I think . . .

References & Resources

Andrade, Heidi L. 2010. "Students as the Definitive Source of Formative Assessment: Academic Self-Assessment and the Self-Regulation of Learning." NERA Conference Proceedings 2010. digitalcommons.lib.uconn.edu/nera_2010/25/.

Biemiller, Andrew, and Donald Meichenbaum. 2017. "The Nature and Nurture of the Self-Directed Learner." In *The Evolution of Cognitive Behavior Therapy*, by Donald Michenbaum. Routledge.

Boch, Françoise, and Anne Piolat. 2005. "Note Taking and Learning: A Summary of Research." *The WAC Journal* 16 (1): 101–113. doi.org/10.37514/WAC-J.2005.16.1.08.

Boud, David, Rosemary Keogh, and David Walker. 2015 [1985]. *Reflection: Turning Experience into Learning.* Routledge.

Breus, Michael. 2024a. "Chronotypes." Sleep Doctor. Updated January 29, 2024. sleepdoctor.com/pages/chronotypes.

Breus, Michael. 2024b. "The Bear Chronotype." Sleep Doctor. Updated January 23, 2024. sleepdoctor.com/pages/chronotypes/bear-chronotype.

Breus, Michael. 2024c. "The Dolphin Chronotype." Sleep Doctor. Updated January 23, 2024. sleepdoctor.com/pages/chronotypes/dolphin-chronotype.

Breus, Michael. 2024d. "The Lion Chronotype." Sleep Doctor. Updated January 23, 2024. sleepdoctor.com/pages/chronotypes/lion-chronotype.

Breus, Michael. 2024e. "The Wolf Chronotype." Sleep Doctor. Updated January 23, 2024. sleepdoctor.com/pages/chronotypes/wolf-chronotype.

Butler, Nadia, Zara Quigg, Rebecca Bates, Lisa Jones, Emma Ashworth, Steve Gowland, and Margaret Jones. 2022. "The Contributing Role of Family, School, and Peer Supportive Relationships in Protecting the Mental Wellbeing of Children and Adolescents." *School Mental Health* 14 (3): 776–788. doi.org/10.1007/s12310-022-09502-9.

Cash, Richard M. 2016. *Self-Regulation in the Classroom: Helping Students Learn How to Learn.* Free Spirit Publishing.

Cash, Richard M. 2017. *Advancing Differentiation: Thinking and Learning for the 21st Century.* Free Spirit Publishing.

CDC (Centers for Disease Control and Prevention). 2024. "Physical Activity Basics: Childhood Activity: An Overview." Published January 8, 2025. Accessed March 24, 2025. cdc.gov/physical-activity-basics/guidelines/children.html.

CDC (Centers for Disease Control and Prevention). 2025. "Physical Activity Boosts Brain Health." Published January 31, 2025. Accessed March 14, 2025. cdc.gov/physical-activity/features/boost-brain-health.html.

Chance, Tyler, and Kristin Petrowske. 2023. "Using AI to Help Students Prepare for the SAT." *Edutopia*, November 9, 2023. edutopia.org/article/using-ai-sat-prep-lessons.

Chang, Bo. 2019. "Reflection in Learning." *Online Learning* 23 (1): 95–110. doi.org/10.24059/olj.v23i1.1447.

Chang, Wan-Chen, and Yu-Min Ku. 2015. "The Effects of Note-Taking Skills Instruction on Elementary Students' Reading." *The Journal of Educational Research* 108 (4): 278–291. doi.org/10.1080/00220671.2014.886175.

Chater, Nick, and Mike Oaksford. 2001. "Human Rationality and the Psychology of Reasoning: Where Do We Go from Here?" *British Journal of Psychology* 92 (1): 193–216. doi.org/10.1348/000712601162031.

Chen, Lang, Se Ri Bae, Christian Battista, Shaozheng Qin, Tianwen Chen, Tanya M. Evans, and Vinod Menon. 2018. "Positive Attitude Toward Math Supports Early Academic Success: Behavioral Evidence and Neurocognitive Mechanisms" *Psychological Science* 29 (3): 390–402. doi.org/10.1177/0956797617735528.

Cheng, Xiaofang. 2023. "Looking Through Goal Theories in Language Learning: A Review on Goal Setting and Achievement Goal Theory." *Frontiers in Psychology* 13: 1035223.

Cherry, Kendra. 2024. "The Components of Attitude: Formation of an Attitude and How It Can Be Changed." Verywell Mind, updated May 5, 2024. verywellmind.com/attitudes-how-they-form-change-shape-behavior-2795897.

Costa, Arthur L., and Bena Kallick. 2008. "Learning Through Reflection." In *Learning and Leading with Habits of Mind,* edited by Arthur L. Costa and Bena Kallick. ASCD.

DeZure, Deborah, Matthew Kaplan, and Martha A. Deerman. 2001. "Research on Student Notetaking: Implications for Faculty and Graduate Student Instructors." *CRLT Occasional Papers* 16: 1–7.

Diwakar Grandhi, Rama Satya. 2018. "The Art and Science of Asking Questions Is the Source of All Knowledge." Medium, March 4, 2018. diwakargrandhi.medium.com/the-art-and-science-of-asking-questions-is-the-source-of-all-knowledge-b49144e2479c.

Dunlosky, John, Katherine A. Rawson, Elizabeth J. Marsh, Mitchell J. Nathan, and Daniel T. Willingham. 2015. "What Works, What Doesn't." *Scientific American Mind* 23 (5): 40–47. doi.org/10.1038/scientificamericangenius0115-40.

Dewey, John. 2022 [1910]. *How We Think.* DigiCat.

Dweck, Carol S. 2006. *Mindset: The New Psychology of Success.* Random House.

Evans, Jonathan St B T, Simon J. Handley, Helen Neilens, and David E. Over. 2007. "Thinking About Conditionals: A Study of Individual Differences." *Memory & Cognition* 35 (7): 1772–1784.

Fallace, Thomas. 2023. "The Long Origins of the Visual, Auditory, and Kinesthetic Learning Style Typology, 1921–2001." *History of Psychology* 26 (4): 334–354. doi.org/10.1037/hop0000240.

Farnam Street Media. n.d. "The Feynman Learning Technique." Accessed March 18. 2025. fs.blog/feynman-learning-technique.

Fernández-Alonso, Rubén, Marcos Álvarez-Díaz, Javier Suárez-Álvarez, and José Muñiz. 2017. "Students' Achievement and Homework Assignment Strategies." *Frontiers in Psychology* 8: 286. doi.org/10.3389/fpsyg.2017.00286.

Friedman, Michael C. 2014. "Notes on Note-Taking: Review of Research and Insights for Students and Instructors." *Harvard Initiative for Learning and Teaching.* hwpi.harvard.edu/files/hilt/files/notetaking_0.pdf.

Galloway, Mollie, Jerusha Conner, and Denise Pope. 2013. "Nonacademic Effects of Homework in Privileged, High-Performing High Schools." *The Journal of Experimental Education* 81 (4): 490–510. doi.org/10.1080/00220973.2012.745469.

Glon, Christina. 2021. "The Pomodoro Technique." Wellness Resources from MacMillan Law Library. Accessed March 18, 2025. guides.libraries.emory.edu/c.php?g=1365627&p=10088719.

Hall, Judith A., Terrence G. Horgan, and Nora A. Murphy. 2019. "Nonverbal Communication." *Annual Review of Psychology* 70: 271–294. doi.org/10.1146/annurev-psych-010418-103145.

Hattie, John. 2016. "Know Thy Impact." In *On Formative Assessment: Readings from Educational Leadership (EL Essentials)*, edited by Marge Scherer. ASCD.

Heacox, Diane, and Richard M. Cash. 2020. *Differentiation for Gifted Learners: Going Beyond the Basics.* Free Spirit Publishing.

Hematian, Fatemeh, Ali Mohammad Rezaei, and Mohammad Ali Mohammadyfar. 2017. "On the Effect of Goal Setting on Self-Directed Learning, Achievement Motivation, and Academic Achievement Among Students." *Modern Applied Science* 11 (1). doi.org/10.5539/mas.v11n1p37.

Hickson, Helen. 2011. "Critical Reflection: Reflecting on Learning to Be Reflective." *Reflective Practice* 12 (6): 829–839. doi.org/10.1080/14623943.2011.616687.

Holden, James, and John S. Schmit. 2002. *Inquiry and the Literary Text: Constructing Discussions in the English Classroom. Classroom Practices in Teaching English.* National Council of Teachers of English.

Hu, Charlotte. 2024. "Why Writing by Hand is Better for Memory and Learning." *Scientific American*, February 21, 2024. scientificamerican.com/article/why-writing-by-hand-is-better-for-memory-and-learning.

Istiqomah, Ni'Matul, Lisa Rokhmani, and Nur Anita Yunikawati. 2022. "How to Prepare Students' Self-Managed Learning in Gregorc's Learning Style." In *Proceedings of the International Conference on Sustainable Innovation on Humanities, Education, and Social Sciences (ICOSI-HESS 2022).* Atlantis Press.

K., Jamie, "How Do I Get the Most Out of Using Tech in the Classroom?" Teachers' Essential Guide to Teaching with Technology from Common Sense Education, September 26, 2023. commonsense.org/education/articles/teachers-essential-guide-to-teaching-with-technology.

KidsHealth. 2021. "Kids and Sleep." Updated January 2021. kidshealth.org/en/parents/sleep.html.

Kobayashi, Keiichi. 2005. "What Limits the Encoding Effect of Note-Taking? A Meta-Analytic Examination." *Contemporary Educational Psychology* 30 (2): 242–262. doi.org/10.1016/j.cedpsych.2004.10.001.

Kobayashi, Keiichi. 2006. "Combined Effects of Note-Taking/-Reviewing on Learning and the Enhancement Through Interventions: A Meta-Analytic Review." *Educational Psychology* 26 (3): 459–477. doi.org/10.1080/01443410500342070.

Kvavik, Robert B. 2005. Convenience, Communications, and Control: How Students Use Technology." *Educating the Net Generation* 1: 7-1.

Luo, Linlin, Kenneth A. Kiewra, and Lydia Samuelson. 2016. "Revising Lecture Notes: How Revision, Pauses, and Partners Affect Note Taking and Achievement." *Instructional Science* 44: 45–67. doi.org/10.1007/s11251-016-9370-4

Lundberg, Carol A. 2003. "The Influence of Time-Limitations, Faculty, and Peer Relationships on Adult Student Learning: A Causal Model." *The Journal of Higher Education* 74 (6): 665–688. doi.org/10.1353/jhe.2003.0045.

Lynch, Tony, and David Mendelsohn. 2010. "Listening." In *An Introduction to Applied Linguistics*, edited by David Coulson, Norbert Schmitt, Jonathon Clenton. Routledge.

Marano, Giuseppe, Georgios D Kotzalidis, Francesco Maria Lisci, Maria Benedetta Anesini, Sara Rossi, Sara Barbonetti, Andrea Cangini, Alice Ronsisvalle, Laura Artuso, Cecilia Falsini, Romina Caso, Giuseppe Mandracchia, Caterina Brisi, Gianandrea Traversi, Osvaldo Mazza, Roberto Pola, Gabriele Sani, Eugenio Maria Mercuri, Eleonora Gaetani, and Marianna Mazza. 2025. "The Neuroscience Behind Writing: Handwriting vs. Typing—Who Wins the Battle?" *Life (Basel)* 15 (3): 345. doi.org10.3390/life15030345.

Martin, Andrew J., and Andrew J. Elliot. 2016. "The Role of Personal Best (PB) Goal Setting in Students' Academic Achievement Gains." *Learning and Individual Differences* 45: 222–227. doi.org/10.1016/j.lindif.2015.12.014.

Medichron Publications. n.d. "Chronobiology: The Science of Time." Accessed March 25, 2025. chronobiology.com/about-chronobiology.

Mendezabal, Marie Jean N. 2013. "Study Habits and Attitudes: The Road to Academic Success." *Open Science Repository Education* 70081928. doi.org/10.7392/Education.70081928.

Moksnes, Unni Karin, and Randi Johansen Reidunsdatter. 2019. "Self-Esteem and Mental Health in Adolescents–Level and Stability During a School Year." *Norsk Epidemiologi* 28 (1-2). doi.org/10.5324/nje.v28i1-2.3052.

Mueller, Pam A., and Daniel M. Oppenheimer. 2014. "The Pen Is Mightier Than the Keyboard: Advantages of Longhand over Laptop Note Taking." *Psychological Science* 25 (6): 1159–1168. doi.org/10.1177/0956797614524581.

National Center for Principled Leadership & Research Ethics. n.d. "Listening and Asking Questions—Quick Tips." ccau.csl.illinois.edu/wp-content/uploads/2023/02/Listening-and-Asking-Questions-Quick-Tips.pdf.

Nomass, Basheer Bassma. 2013. "The Impact of Using Technology in Teaching English as a Second Language." *English Language and Literature Studies* 3 (1): 111. doi.org/ 10.5539/ells.v3n1p111.

Ogut, Eren, Yesim Senol, and Fatos B. Yildirim. 2017. "Do Learning Styles Affect Study Duration and Academic Success?" *European Journal of Anatomy* 21 (3): 235–240.

Pashler, Harold, Mark A. McDaniel, Doug Rohrer, and Robert A. Bjork. 2008. "Learning Styles: Concepts and Evidence". *Psychological Science in the Public Interest* 9 (3): 105–119. doi.org/10.1111/j.1539-6053.2009.01038.x.

Pauk, Walter. 1989. *How to Study in College: Instructor's Manual with Test Items.* Houghton Mifflin.

Pauk, Walter, and Ross J. Q. Owens. 2010. "The Cornell System: Take Effective Notes." In *How to Study in College (10 ed.).* Wadsworth.

Peverly, Stephen T., Vivek Ramaswamy, Cindy Brown, James F. Sumowski, Moona Alidoost, and Joanna K. Garner. 2007. "What Predicts Skill in Lecture Note Taking?" *Journal of Educational Psychology* 99 (1): 167–180.

Piolat, Annie, Thierry Olive, and Ronald T. Kellogg. 2005. "Cognitive Effort During Note Taking." *Applied Cognitive Psychology* 19 (3): 291–312. doi.org/10.1002/acp.1086.

Rice, Tom. 2015. "Listening." In *Keywords in Sound*, edited by David Novak and Matt Sakakeeny. Duke University Press.

Rodgers, Carol. 2002. "Defining Reflection: Another Look at John Dewey and Reflective Thinking." *Teachers College Record* 104 (4): 842–866. doi.org/10.1111/1467-9620.00181.

Rogers, Carl. 1951. *Client-Centered Therapy: Its Current Practice, Implications, and Theory.* Constable.

Said-Metwaly, Sameh, Belén Fernández-Castilla, Eva Kyndt, and Wilm Van den Noortgate. 2020. "Testing Conditions and Creative Performance: Meta-Analyses of the Impact of Time Limits and Instructions." *Psychology of Aesthetics, Creativity, and the Arts* 14 (1): 15–38. doi.org/10.1037/aca0000244.

Savas, Victoriana. 2023. "Strategies for Supporting Student Goal-Setting," *Edutopia*, April 24, 2023. edutopia.org/article/supporting-student-goal-setting.

Schoolcues. 2022. "7 Goal-Setting Strategies for Students." *Schoolcues* blog, April 6, 2022. schoolcues.com/blog/7-goal-setting-strategies-for-students.

Schaeffer, Nora Cate, and Stanley Presser. 2003. "The Science of Asking Questions." *Annual Review of Sociology* 29 (1): 65–88. doi.org/10.1146/annurev.soc.29.110702.110112.

Schunk, Dale H., and Carol A. Mullen. 2012. "Self-Efficacy as an Engaged Learner." In *Handbook of Research on Student Engagement*, edited by Sandra L. Christenson, Amy L. Reschly, and Cathy Wylie. Springer.

Silver, Harvey F., Joyce W. Jackson, and Daniel R. Moirao. 2011. *Task Rotation Strategies for Differentiating Activities and Assessments by Learning Style.* ASCD.

Small, Marian. 2012. *Good Questions: Great Ways to Differentiate Mathematics Instruction.* Teachers College Press.

Stacy, Elizabeth Moore, and Jeff Cain. 2015. "Note-Taking and Handouts in the Digital Age." *American Journal of Pharmaceutical Education* 79 (7): 107. doi.org/10.5688/ajpe797107.

Stanovich, Keith E., and Richard F. West. 1997. "Reasoning Independently of Prior Belief and Individual Differences in Actively Open-Minded Thinking." *Journal of Educational Psychology* 89 (2): 342–357. doi.org/10.1037/0022-0663.89.2.342.

Stein, Elizabeth. 2015. "5 Aids to Help Students Set Learning Goals." *MiddleWeb*, January 18, 2015. middleweb.com/20021/5-aids-help-students-set-learning-goals.

Sternberg, Robert, and Elena Grigorenko. 2007. *Teaching for Successful Intelligence: To Increase Student Learning and Achievement*, second edition. Corwin Press.

Strauss, Valerie. 2016. "A Telling Experiment Reveals a Big Problem Among College Students: They Don't Know How to Study." *Washington Post*, September 14, 2016. washingtonpost.com/news/answer-sheet/wp/2016/09/14/a-telling-experiment-reveals-a-big-problem-among-college-students-they-dont-know-how-to-study.

Sundre, Donna L. 2000. "Motivation Scale Background and Scoring Guide." James Madison University Center for Assessment and Research Studies. jmu.edu/assessment/_files/pdf/sos_scoring_guide.pdf.

Tamim, Rana M., Robert M. Bernard, Eugene Borokhovski, Philip C. Abrami, and Richard F. Schmid. 2011. "What Forty Years of Research Says About the Impact of Technology on Learning: A Second-Order Meta-Analysis and Validation Study." *Review of Educational Research* 81 (1): 4–28. doi.org/10.3102/0034654310393361.

Texas A&M University. n.d. "Reading Strategies: The SQ3R Method." The Academic Success Center. Accessed March 18, 2025. asc.tamu.edu/study-learning-handouts/reading-strategies-the-sq3r-method.

Thompson, Jeff. 2011. "Is Nonverbal Communication a Numbers Game?" *Psychology Today*, September 30, 2011. psychologytoday.com/us/blog/beyond-words/201109/is-nonverbal-communication-a-numbers-game.

Trautwein, Ulrich. 2007. "The Homework–Achievement Relation Reconsidered: Differentiating Homework Time, Homework Frequency, and Homework Effort." *Learning and Instruction* 17 (3): 372–388. doi.org/10.1016/j.learninstruc.2007.02.009.

Tus, Jhoselle, Francis Rayo, Reymark Lubo, and Mark Anthony Cruz. 2020. "The Learners' Study Habits and Its Relation on Their Academic Performance." *International Journal of All Research Writings* 2 (6): 1–19. doi.org/10.6084/m9.figshare.13325177.v1.

USDA Nutrition.gov. n.d. "Healthy Eating." Accessed March 14, 2025. nutrition.gov/topics/basic-nutrition/healthy-eating.

Vollrath, Daniel. 2022. "5 Strategies to Improve Students' Listening Skills." *Edutopia*, October 7, 2022. edutopia.org/article/5-strategies-improve-students-listening-skills.

Voyer, Daniel. 2011. "Time Limits and Gender Differences on Paper-and-Pencil Tests on Mental Rotation: A Meta-Analysis." *Psychonomic Bulletin & Review* 18 (2): 267–277. doi.org/10.3758/s13423-010-0042-0.

Walck-Shannon, Elise M., Shaina F. Rowell, and Regina F. Frey. 2021. "To What Extent Do Study Habits Relate to Performance?" *CBE—Life Sciences Education* 20 (1): ar6. doi.org/10.1187/cbe.20-05-0091.

Whelan, Jesse. 2019. "Using the Leitner System to Improve Your Study." *Medium*, May 7, 2019. jessewhelan.medium.com/using-the-leitner-system-to-improve-your-study-d5edafae7f0.

Willingham, Daniel T. 2023. *Outsmart Your Brain: Why Learning Is Hard and How You Can Make It Easy.* Simon and Schuster.

World Health Organization. 1994. "Adolescent Health and Development: The Key to the Future." Global Commission on Women's Health. iris.who.int/handle/10665/62550.

World Health Organization. 2024. "Physical Activity." June 26, 2024. who.int/news-room/fact-sheets/detail/physical-activity.

Index

Digital Resources

Accessing the Digital Resources

The digital resources can be downloaded by following these steps:

1. Go to www.tcmpub.com/digital
2. Use the ISBN number to redeem the digital resources.
3. Respond to the question using the book.
4. Follow the prompts on the Content Cloud website to sign in or create a new account.
5. The content redeemed will now be on your My Content screen. Click on the product to look through the digital resources. All resources are available for download. Select files can be previewed, opened, and shared.

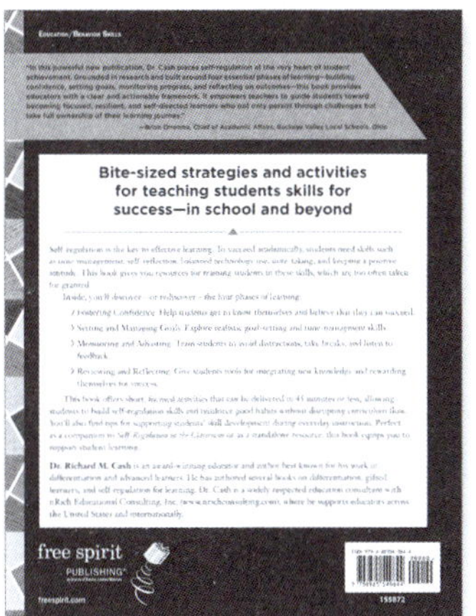

For questions and assistance with your ISBN redemption, please contact Teacher Created Materials.
email: customerservice@tcmpub.com
phone: 800-858-7339

Contents of the Digital Resources

The Digital Resources include digital versions of all of the student pages and forms in this book.

About the Author

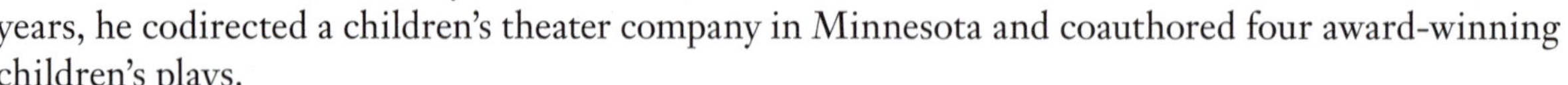

Dr. Richard M. Cash is an award-winning author and educator who has worked in the field of education for more than three decades.

His range of experience includes teaching, curriculum coordination, and program administration. Currently, he is an internationally recognized education consultant. His consulting work has taken him throughout the United States, as well as into Canada, the Czech Republic, China, England, Indonesia, the Kingdom of Saudi Arabia, Mexico, Oman, Poland, Qatar, Spain, South Korea, and Turkey.

Richard received his doctorate in educational leadership and a master's degree in curriculum and instruction from the University of St. Thomas in Minneapolis, Minnesota. Along with his bachelor's degree in education from the University of Minnesota, Richard holds a bachelor's degree in theater from the University of Wisconsin, Eau Claire. For over ten years, he codirected a children's theater company in Minnesota and coauthored four award-winning children's plays.

He was the recipient of the National Association for Gifted Children's Early Leader Award (2011), recognizing his leadership in programming for gifted children. Richard was also named the "Friend of the Gifted, 2016" by Minnesota Educators of the Gifted and Talented. His areas of expertise are educational programming, rigorous and challenging curriculum design, differentiated instruction, 21st-century skills, brain-compatible classrooms, gifted and talented education, and self-regulated learning.

Richard is the author of *Advancing Differentiation: Thinking and Learning for the 21st Century* (2017), a finalist for the Association for Educational Publishers Distinguished Achievement Award and winner of the The Legacy Book® Award; *Self-Regulation in the Classroom: Helping Students Learn How to Learn* (2016); and coauthor (with Diane Heacox) of *Differentiation for Gifted Learners: Going Beyond the Basics* (2020), winner of The Legacy Book® Award.

Richard lives in Palm Springs, California.